CARING FOR YOU AND YOUR BABY

CARING FOR YOU AND YOUR BABY

From Pregnancy through the First Year of Life

By Fairview Health Services
Affiliated with the University of Minnesota

Fairview Press
Minneapolis

Published by Fairview Press, 2450 Riverside Avenue South, Minneapolis, MN 55434.

Library of Congress Cataloging-in-Publication Data
Caring for you and your baby : from pregnancy through the first year of
    life / by Fairview Health Services, affiliated with the University of
    Minnesota.
            p.   cm.
        Includes index.
        ISBN 1-57749-052-5 (alk. paper)
        1. Pregnancy. 2. Infants--Care. I. Fairview Health Services.
    RG525.C346   1997
    618.2'4--dc21   97-22621
                                                                         CIP

First printing: October 1997
Printed in the United States of America

00 99 98 97   5 4 3 2 1

Editor: Linda Picone
Book Designer: Jane Dahms
Illustrator: Barbara Beshoar
Cover Designer: Laurie Duren

For a free catalog of Fairview Press books, call toll-free 1-800-544-8207.
Or visit our website at www.Press.Fairview.org.

Acknowledgments

Fairview is a community-focused health system providing a complete range of services, from prevention of illness and injury to care for the most complex medical conditions. The information contained in this book was assembled and developed by our maternal and newborn services department.

This book is a direct response to feedback from our patients and their families. Delivering over 11,000 babies each year, Fairview cares for more moms and babies than any other health care provider in the state of Minnesota.

Many individuals from Fairview Health Services contributed to this project. They include Nancy Barkley, RN; Deb Cathcart, RN, MS; Lora Harding-Dundek, BA, MPH, ICCE; Kathy Eide, RN, NP; Mary Ess, RN; Patricia Fontaine, MD; Becky Gams, RN; Margaret Harder, CCRN, BSN, MA; Jeanne Hartwig, LPN, ICCE; Debra Heaver, RN; Kathryn Kerber, RN, MS, CNS; Jane Lowe, RN, IBCLC; Rachel McCann, RN; Laurie McNamara; Kathleen Maloney, RN; Bonnie Miller, RN; Kim Mullon, RN; Sue Nesheim, RN; Jeri Price, BA, CCE; Jane Rauenhorst, MALP; Marie Root, RN, IBCLE; Anthony Shibley, MD; Arlyce Shook, RNC; Noreen Siebenaler, RN, MSN, IBCLC; Patti Sollinger, MSN, CPNF; and Aner Vladaver, MD.

We thank our patients and their families and the many other people who helped move this book from conception to reality.

Contents

Introduction

Maybe you were pretty sure before you went to see your health care provider. Your breasts were bigger, you felt a little sick to your stomach, you'd been trying to get pregnant. Or maybe you hadn't thought about it at all—you'd been using birth control, you were still having periods, you were convinced you *couldn't* be pregnant.

Whether it's a surprise or not, you've just learned you're going to have a baby. Millions of women have had babies, so it's no big deal, right?

Wrong. This is *your* pregnancy, *your* baby, *your* life. It's special.

If this is your first baby, you may be unsure about what to expect during your pregnancy, when the baby is born, and when you become a parent. Your friends and relatives tell stories, some scary and some encouraging. There are hundreds of books about having babies. Which is right for you?

Caring for You and Your Baby gives the basics of pregnancy and birth, and how to care for your baby during his or her first 15 months of life. If this is the only book you look at, you will have a good start on knowing what to expect.

If you want to read more, at the end of most chapters you'll find a list of books you might find helpful.

If this is not your first baby, you may be familiar with much of the information in this book. Use it as a reminder about things like eating well, exercising safely, learning how to breathe properly when giving birth, and what to expect when you deliver.

You will see the words "health care provider" used often throughout this book. We believe that you will have a better pregnancy and a healthier baby if you and your health care providers—who may be physicians, nurses, nurse practitioners, certified nurse-midwives, childbirth educators, or others—work together. You should always tell your health care provider the truth about what you are doing and feeling, and you should expect honest, clear answers to your questions in return.

The advice offered in this book is widely accepted in the health care community, but if your health care provider tells you something different, you should follow your health care provider's advice. Your health care provider knows you better than any book can.

Whether you're concerned about a strange pain in the middle of the night or wondering how long you can continue to jog, your health care provider is the one who can provide the answers you need.

When in doubt, talk to your health care provider.

1 *You're Pregnant*

Throughout your pregnancy you will need to pay special attention to your health, for both your sake and your baby's sake. Exercise, diet, and other habits are important to how you feel during the pregnancy and to giving your baby the best start in life.

The next sections will take you through your entire pregnancy and the birth of your baby. The chapters are ordered in the way your pregnancy will proceed, so you can turn to each chapter to read about how your body is changing, how your baby is developing, and what you may be feeling.

**SOME OF THE QUESTIONS ANSWERED
IN THIS CHAPTER INCLUDE:**

- What can I expect from my health care provider?
- How can I get the most from clinic visits?
- Can I drink alcohol while I'm pregnant?
- What should I eat?
- How much weight should I gain?
- Can I exercise?
- Why am I so moody?
- What if I feel overwhelmed?
- Is sex safe during pregnancy?

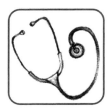

YOU AND YOUR HEALTH CARE PROVIDER

THE HEALTH CARE PROVIDERS at your clinic can help you have a better pregnancy and a healthier baby—if you start seeing them as soon as you think you are pregnant. It is important to follow their recommendations as the months go by.

You may choose a doctor, a nurse practitioner, or a nurse midwife as your primary care provider during your pregnancy.

- Your **doctor** may be an **obstetrician**, who specializes in caring for women through pregnancy and birth, or a **family practice physician**, who can provide most health care for all members of a family.

- **Certified nurse-midwives** are registered nurses with training in pregnancy and childbirth. They provide complete prenatal care, deliver babies, and perform well-woman visits, including pap smears and family planning. Certified nurse-midwives work closely with obstetricians and will work with you as a partner in your care.

- **Nurse practitioners** are registered nurses who have had special training in women's health. They often work with doctors during a pregnancy, and you may see a nurse practitioner frequently during your clinic visits. They do not deliver babies, but they are responsible for routine care before and after birth.

- **Physician's Assistants (PAs)** have special medical training to help doctors provide care in many different areas, including pregnancy and childbirth.

At first, you probably will visit the clinic once a month or so. Later in your pregnancy, you will be asked to come in more often, since things may change very quickly at that point. Your blood pressure, urine, and weight will be checked each time you come to the clinic. As the baby develops, its growth, heart rate, and position in your body also will be checked.

The visits to the clinic will help most women feel comfortable with their health and their baby's health. But if there are any complications, these regular visits will let your health care

What can I expect from my health care provider?

provider find them early, which is always important in preventing and treating problems.

Your health care providers are the experts when it comes to pregnancies, but you are the expert when it comes to *you*. Don't be afraid to tell them what you're thinking or feeling or worrying about. They need to know. Think of yourself and your health care providers as a team, working together toward a successful pregnancy and a healthy baby.

To make sure your visits to the clinic are most helpful, you should:

Write down any questions you have before your visit.

Keep a notebook or a writing pad handy. When you think of a question, write it down. Then, when you visit the clinic, you won't forget it.

Ask again if you don't understand an answer.

Medical words and phrases can sound odd or even frightening to patients. Repeat any question, or parts of it, if you don't understand the answer. Your health care providers want to make sure you get the information you need.

Be honest.

It's very, very important that you level with your health care providers about your activities—including the ones that may embarrass you. If you smoke or use drugs or alcohol, be honest. Your health care providers will help with education and referrals.

Describe how you're feeling as clearly as you can.

Don't just say "it hurts"; say *where*, and *how much*, and *how often*, and *when*. Sometimes it's not easy to describe, but try to be specific.

Keep track of what you learn during office visits.

Take notes during your office visits. It's easy to forget what you've just heard, or to get confused when you get a lot of information at once. Write it down. Keep a chart of your weight, blood pressure, and other tests (see the middle of this book for a place to do this).

How can I get the most from clinic visits?

Get more information.

Bookstores and libraries contain many excellent books on having a baby. At the end of each chapter in this book, you'll find a list of books, videos, and other resources you might find helpful.

WHAT YOU HAVE A RIGHT TO EXPECT

Your health care providers should give you good medical services in a respectful manner. This includes:

- **Prompt service.** You can expect to spend some time in the waiting room, but let the staff know—calmly—if you feel that you've been sitting too long. Also, expect your health care provider to return telephone calls in a reasonable time.
- **Respectful treatment.** You and your health care providers should have an open, honest, friendly, and respectful relationship. If you feel that you are not being treated respectfully, talk about it with your health care provider.
- **Strict regard for confidentiality.** Your visits to the health care provider and your discussions with him or her are private. Your health care provider will not talk about you with any other patients.
- **Sensitivity to cultural differences.** We're not all alike in our beliefs and habits, but your health care providers should understand and respect your cultural and ethnic background. If there are misunderstandings, it may be simply that your health care provider is not familiar with your culture. You can help educate him or her.

NUTRITION AND HEALTH

YOUR BABY deserves a healthy start. Eating right, staying away from harmful substances, and exercising regularly during your pregnancy are good for your baby—and for you.

SMOKING

Even if you know someone who smoked through her pregnancy and who has a healthy baby, the evidence is clear: Smoking is bad for babies. If you smoke, being pregnant is the best reason in the world to stop. Women who smoke during their pregnancy are more likely to have babies that are premature, weigh less than 5½ pounds, or are stillborn or die as infants. These are frightening facts. Why take a chance with your baby? Your health care provider can help you with a program to quit smoking.

ALCOHOL

"But my mother drank while she was pregnant with me and I turned out fine," you may say. It's hard to believe that something that is so much a part of our lives—a beer at a ball game, a glass of wine with dinner, champagne to celebrate a special occasion—can be dangerous to your unborn baby.

Drinking during pregnancy can cause **Fetal Alcohol Syndrome (FAS)**, a combination of birth defects that includes mental retardation. Fetal Alcohol Syndrome is the leading cause of retardation in the United States.

No one knows exactly how much alcohol during pregnancy is too much. Some studies have shown that even a small amount on a regular basis can affect the growth of a baby. Why take chances? The Surgeon General has recommended that pregnant women not drink *any* alcohol.

If you have had an occasional drink—maybe before you knew you were pregnant—you probably don't need to worry. However, you should talk to your health care provider, just to make sure.

CAFFEINE

There is no evidence that caffeine causes birth defects, but heavy coffee drinkers may have smaller babies. It's best if you drink no more than 2 or 3 cups of coffee or tea or cans of soda with caffeine (like colas) a day. Chocolate also contains caffeine.

Is it okay to smoke while I'm pregnant?

Can I drink alcohol while I'm pregnant?

DRUGS

Any drugs, whether illegal substances like marijuana, prescription drugs, or even over-the-counter medications as ordinary as aspirin, can have an effect on your baby. You need to talk honestly with your health care giver about what kinds of medications or drugs you take.

Most illegal drugs, including cocaine, heroin, speed, downers, LSD, and PCP, can seriously harm your baby during pregnancy. They may cause long-term effects, including mental, physical, and emotional problems for the new baby.

Over-the-counter medications and prescription drugs may be safe, but you need to ask your health care provider about them to be sure. Some things, such as aspirin, that are usually just fine, can be dangerous when you're pregnant. Make a list of everything you take, from vitamins to prescribed antibiotics to pain relievers, and share it with your health care provider.

Herbal remedies may also have an effect on your body or your baby. If you use herbs as medicine, check with your health care provider for safety recommendations.

EATING RIGHT

There will be times, during your pregnancy, when you'll feel like eating everything in sight, and other times when the thought of food will make your stomach lurch.

Whether you're eating a lot or a little, you should eat the right foods. Pregnancy is a good time to develop healthy eating habits, for yourself and for your growing family.

The Food Pyramid shown here gives the essentials of a healthy diet. A pregnant or nursing mother needs plenty of calcium, and should have at least 3 to 4 servings of dairy products each day. If you don't like milk, try yogurt or cottage cheese.

In addition to calcium, pregnant women need folic acid, which has been shown to reduce the occurrence of some birth defects. Folic acid, a compound in the vitamin B family, can be found in leafy green vegetables, fresh fruit, liver, food yeasts, and peanuts, or can be taken a supplement.

Here's what different kinds of food do for you and your baby:

The Food Pyramid

The pyramid is a guide of what to eat each day. Try to eat more of the foods in the bottom three parts of the pyramid. You need food from every group each day to have a well-balanced diet.

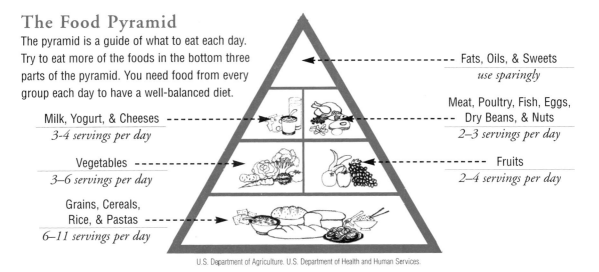

Fats, Oils, & Sweets
use sparingly

Meat, Poultry, Fish, Eggs, Dry Beans, & Nuts
2–3 servings per day

Milk, Yogurt, & Cheeses
3-4 servings per day

Vegetables
3–6 servings per day

Fruits
2–4 servings per day

Grains, Cereals, Rice, & Pastas
6–11 servings per day

U.S. Department of Agriculture. U.S. Department of Health and Human Services.

- **Dairy products** (milk, cheese, yogurt)—help build strong bones and teeth.
- **Protein** (meat, fish, eggs, soybeans, nuts, peanut butter)—aids brain and organ development.
- **Citrus** (oranges, grapefruit, lemon juice)—builds strong body cells and blood.
- **Leafy green vegetables** (spinach, broccoli, cabbage)—help your baby's bones, hair, and skin develop properly.
- **Other fruits and vegetables** (potatoes, carrots, apples, grapes, berries)—help prevent constipation and give you energy.
- **Bread, cereal, pasta, carbohydrates**—promote nervous system development.
- **Water and other fluids** (but not sodas or coffee)—8 to10 glasses or more each day prevent dehydration.

What should I eat?

When you're hungry, you may be tempted to reach for snacks like cookies, cake, or ice cream. Your body is telling you that it wants to eat, but it isn't telling you what to eat. You decide that, and you can make healthy decisions.

Keep healthy snacks handy. An orange can give you a sense of being full, and it's good for you and your baby. A glass of apple juice is better than a can of soda; plain crackers are better than potato chips. (Crackers, cereal, and toast often help with nausea.)

WEIGHT GAIN

You are going to gain weight when you're pregnant, and you need to for your baby's healthy development. You may not like the way you look, especially if you've worked hard to keep a slim figure. Remember that a healthy pregnant woman looks different than a healthy *non*-pregnant woman.

If you are underweight, you will need to gain more (28 to 40 pounds) than if you are overweight (15 to 25 pounds). Average-weight women should gain 25 to 35 pounds. Eat sensibly and you should gain the amount that's right for you. An extra 300 calories a day over a healthy non-pregnant diet is just about right.

During the first three months, you may gain only a few pounds (3 to 6), most of it from the increase in your blood and fluids. During the rest of your pregnancy, you may gain as much as a pound a week, as the baby grows.

Average Weight Gain

A weight gain of 25 to 35 pounds during pregnancy is average. Part of this weight comes as the baby grows inside you (7 1/2 to 8 1/2 pounds) and the rest as your body changes to allow the baby to grow and as it prepares for breastfeeding the baby after birth.

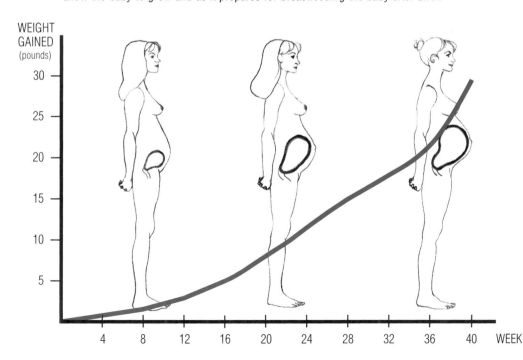

EXERCISE

REGULAR EXERCISE during pregnancy is not only good for your baby, it will help you feel better, too. It will give you energy, make you feel better about yourself, reduce stress—and help you get back in shape faster after the baby is born.

Can I exercise?

If you already exercise regularly, you can probably continue what you are doing, but at a slower pace, until your baby is born. Check with your health care provider if your regular exercise is extremely strenuous or involves jarring movements. If something starts to feel uncomfortable, pay attention to the signal your body is sending and substitute another kind of exercise.

If you have not been exercising regularly, start gradually and don't suddenly try to do anything too strenuous. Walking briskly for 30 minutes or more, at least 3 times a week, is excellent exercise.

Consult with your health care provider before starting any exercise program. Whatever exercises you do, make your movements flowing, rather than sharp or punching. Stop if you feel pain. And always remember to drink plenty of water.

The following exercises are particularly good for pregnant women.

Kegel

Deliberately squeeze together the muscles you use when you stop a stream of urine. (One way to do this: Imagine that you are sitting on the toilet and the phone rings.) Hold the squeeze for a few seconds, then release. Do this as often as possible, even 100 times a day. You can do Kegels anywhere. Doing Kegels will increase the tone of your pelvic floor muscles, which will be especially important when your baby puts pressure on your bladder. It will decrease your chances of leaking urine when you cough or sneeze. It can enhance lovemaking, too. It's the most important exercise for pregnant women.

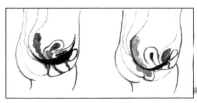

STRONG PELVIC
FLOOR MUSCLE

WEAK PELVIC
FLOOR MUSCLE

Pelvic Rock

Get on your hands and knees. Look at your knees, pull your hips in, and arch your back like an angry cat. Hold the position for a few seconds (try counting to 5), then release. Repeat at least 10 times. This exercise helps stretch out your lower back at the end of a long day of standing.

Don't let your back arch or your tummy sag in this position.

Tailor Sit

Sit in a butterfly position with feet touching. Put your arms between your legs and drop your knees toward the floor. Count to 10, then release. Repeat at least 10 times. This exercise strengthens and stretches your inner thigh muscles.

Try not to slouch. Your lower back should remain straight.

Shoulder Rotation

Put your arms straight out and make circles at your sides. Rotate 5 times in one direction, then 5 in the other direction. You can also do shoulder rotations with your hands touching your shoulders. These exercises will relieve tension in your upper back if you work at a desk or computer all day.

Try to concentrate on perfect posture while doing rotations. Keep the rest of your body still as you move your arms.

Feet should be about shoulder-width apart.

Back Flattening

Lie on your back with your arms at your sides. Pull your knees to your chest and cross your ankles. Press the small of your back to the floor and rotate your hips. Make circles in one direction for a few moments, then in the reverse direction. The exercise should not be done after 20 weeks of pregnancy, but in the first few months it can help relieve backaches.

Keep breathing while doing any exercise(s). It is important for you and your baby to keep air circulating through your bodies.

YOUR EMOTIONS

BEING PREGNANT and having a baby will change your life in ways you may not be able to imagine. It's normal to have a lot of different feelings and different moods throughout your pregnancy. Sometimes you will feel happy, on top of the world. At other times you will burst into tears at the smallest thing. You may be impatient and irritable one moment, mellow and peaceful another. Sometimes you'll feel everything—happy, sad, irritable, peaceful—almost at the same time.

Some of these mood swings are the result of hormonal changes. It helps to remember that they are normal.

Having a good sense of humor about it all will help you, and those around you. Think of having this baby as an adventure, and enjoy the changes in your body and your outlook on life.

Physical changes can affect your mood. If you're feeling nauseous and tired during the first months of your pregnancy, for example, it's likely that you're going to be a bit touchy, too. When your body is bigger and you have a hard time getting out of a chair toward the end of your pregnancy, you may feel impatient, as if the baby will never be born.

If this is your first baby, you may be unsure of just what having a baby will mean to you. Some questions you and your partner may wonder about include: Is my home big enough? Will I need to give up my job? Can I take care of a baby by myself? What will labor and delivery be like? Do I have enough money? Will I love my baby enough? Will my baby love me? Talking about these issues together will help relieve anxiety and let you laugh at the silly questions while finding answers to the serious questions.

If you've had children already, you may be more confident about some things—you know how to change a diaper and feed a baby, for example—but there will be other concerns. Do I have enough energy for another child? How is my partner going to react? Will my other children resent this baby? Do I have enough love to go around?

Why am I so moody?

During the first three months of your pregnancy, you're likely to look inward, to feel protective of the baby inside you and to think about what he or she is going to mean to your life. The second three months are often a period of looking outward. Your pregnancy shows, you feel good physically, and you're likely to be excited about it all. Then the last three months are another period of looking inward. The weight of your baby may be slowing you down a bit, and you know that it's only a short time until you will have a child to care for.

For some women, it helps to write fears and happy thoughts in a journal during their pregnancy. Some find that just talking to other mothers relieves much of their anxiety. Some read everything they can about having a baby because being well-informed makes them feel more confident.

If this pregnancy was unplanned, if you don't have a caring partner or a support system, or if you are planning to place your baby for adoption, you will need extra emotional support. Talk to your health care provider, who can direct you to agencies and groups that will help.

STRESS

You can cope better with the stress in your life—including the stress of being pregnant—if you:

- *Eat a healthy, well-balanced diet.*
- *Get enough sleep.* Listen to what your body tells you; take a nap when you need to.
- *Get regular exercise and fresh air.*
- *Pace yourself.* Take time to relax. Don't try to do everything.
- *Enjoy yourself.* Do at least one thing every day that makes you feel good.
- *Let others help you.* Your partner or others may offer to take care of the things you normally do. Let them.
- *If you are having trouble handling the stress in your life, talk to your health care provider, who can help you find support in the clinic, hospital, or community.*

What if I feel
overwhelmed?

Your Partner

Your partner's life is changing, too. Preparing for this baby together can be a wonderful experience, but it can also mean a time of working through issues that you may not have discussed before. You have a right to expect support and some special attention during your pregnancy, but remember that your partner has emotional needs, too. Often partners don't feel the reality of the pregnancy as quickly as the woman whose body is changing.

Communication is essential. Talk about what you are feeling and listen to your partner's feelings. Set aside time for the two of you during the pregnancy so that you can share your excitement and your fears in an unstressed, unrushed way.

Sexuality

Is sex safe during pregnancy ?

For most normal pregnancies, it's safe to have sex, even up through the last few weeks before the baby is born. But you, or your partner, may find your interest in sex changing during the pregnancy.

You may not be very interested in sex during the first three months of your pregnancy simply because your breasts are sore or you're tired or nauseated. During the second three months, you are likely to have more energy and you may feel very sexy with your enlarged breasts and more sensitive genital area. In the last three months of pregnancy, the size of the baby may make sexual intercourse seem awkward.

Your partner's interest in sex may mirror your own; when you feel positive and interested, your partner is likely to feel the same. Some partners find a pregnant woman to be lovely and sensuous in their growing body. But sometimes your partner may have other fears or concerns. Will sex hurt the baby? Are you now a mother and not a lover?

What matters is how you feel and how your partner feels. Now is an important time for you to be gentle and considerate with each other. If one of you is interested in sex and the other is not, you can explore other ways of being intimate, from massage or cuddling to touching until you have an orgasm.

In some situations, your health care provider may advise you not to have intercourse, or to restrict the kind of sex you have. These situations include:

- **A history of miscarriage.**
- **Vaginal infection.**
- **Vaginal or abdominal pain.**
- **Vaginal bleeding.**
- **A possibility of preterm labor.**
- **Membranes that have ruptured or are leaking.**

DOMESTIC ABUSE

IT CAN BE hard to leave a relationship, even if you are being emotionally or physically abused. You may worry about whether you can support yourself without your partner, or you may worry about being lonely. Now that you're pregnant, you may wonder if you could raise a child without a partner.

Pregnancy sometimes increases the abuse by a partner. It is reported that 25 to 40 percent of all abused women are abused during pregnancy. There can be many reasons for this, but none of them are an excuse for harm to a woman and her baby.

If you are in a relationship that is abusive, even if your partner only loses control "once in a while," you need to think about your baby as well as yourself now. Abused pregnant women are more likely to have complications during their pregnancies, including miscarriage, babies with low birth weight, hemorrhaging, early labor, and the unborn baby's death.

No one deserves to be abused. Not you or your baby. (Or your partner: Occasionally, women abuse their partners. If you find yourself violent and out of control with your partner, you need to stop and seek help.)

There are many agencies and services to help you—and your partner—avoid abuse and create a safe environment for your baby. Talk to your health care provider for a referral.

WARNING SIGNS

WHEN YOU'RE pregnant, some of the changes in your body can feel very strange. Most of the time these changes are a normal part of pregnancy, even if they're different than anything you've felt before. But sometimes they can be signs of problems.

Tell your health care provider if at anytime during your pregnancy you see or feel:

- **Change in your vaginal discharge.** This means *any* bleeding from the vagina, or an increase in vaginal discharge before the 36th week (or about a month before your baby is due).
- **Sudden decrease in the baby's movement.** Your clinic may teach you how to count your baby's movements. A page to keep track of your baby's kicking and other movements is included in the Keeping Track part of this book.
- **Sharp abdominal pain, or pain that doesn't seem to go away.**
- **Unusual health problems.** These can include:

  Severe nausea, vomiting or headache.
  Swelling of hands or face, or very noticeable swelling of feet or ankles.
  Blurred vision, seeing spots in front of your eyes.
  Pain or a burning feeling when you urinate.
  A decrease in the amount of urine you pass.
  Chills or fever.

- **A feeling that something isn't quite right.** Even if you can't figure out exactly what it is, trust your body and your instincts.

GENETIC COUNSELING AND TESTING

GENETIC COUNSELING and testing helps families know more
about whether they are likely to have a child with birth defects.
They also can help find a pattern of genetic disorders in your
family, if there is one. Genetic counseling and testing is not
routine, but your health care provider may feel that it's recommended, especially if:

- **You are 35 or older.**
- **You have had a child with a birth defect.**
- **Your family has a medical history of genetic disorders.**

Usually, genetic testing is recommended *before* you decide to
have a baby if there is a concern that you or the baby's father
may carry a particular genetic condition, or if there is any family
history of genetic disorders.

After you become pregnant, genetic counseling and testing
may be suggested as you make decisions about the pregnancy
and care of your baby after he or she is born.

An increased risk for having a baby with certain birth
defects, such as Down Syndrome or spina bifida, can be shown
by testing a sample of the pregnant woman's blood. If the blood
sample indicates an increased risk, the health care provider may
recommend an ultrasound exam for a more definite result. For
further testing, your health care provider may suggest an amniocentesis. An **amniocentesis** is the withdrawal of a small amount
of the amniotic fluid that surrounds your baby. This fluid can be
tested in a laboratory to give more accurate information about
your baby and any genetic health risks.

If genetic tests are recommended, your health care provider will
tell you how they will be done and if there are risks to your baby so
you can make an informed decision. Keep in mind that most
babies are born with no serious birth defects. Even when a risk
of a birth defect is found, a normal pregnancy is still most likely.

FOR PARTNERS

YOU MAY BE as excited and happy as your pregnant partner. Maybe you're even *more* excited and happy. You and your partner are entering a new stage of your relationship. It means a chance to make the relationship even stronger.

You might also feel a little overwhelmed. You are expected to be supportive of your partner, but you may have your own doubts and fears to contend with.

Try to remember the good feelings you have. Preparing for a baby can be a way to grow closer. Make sure you talk to your partner. Tell her about your hopes and dreams for the baby and for both of you. Then be sure to listen to what she's telling you as well. She's likely to be going through many emotions throughout the pregnancy. Enjoy the good times and be patient with any blue periods.

Keep your sense of humor, but make sure you're laughing *with* your partner, not at her. She can burst into tears at the slightest comment. Don't take it personally.

Sex can be a tricky issue during pregnancy. You may be interested when she's not, or she may be interested when you're not. Be patient, and think of ways to be close if you aren't having intercourse.

Be supportive of your partner's developing healthy habits, and join her in them. Eat well with her, exercise with her, stop drinking. If you smoke, now is the time to stop. Secondhand smoke is harmful to both mother and baby. Every baby deserves to come into a healthy home.

FOR MORE INFORMATION

A Child is Born by Lennart Nilsson.
Active Birth by Janet Balaskas.
The Birth Partner by Penny Simkin.
Essential Exercises for the Childbearing Year by Elizabeth Noble.
Pregnancy, Childbirth and the Newborn by Penny Simkin and others.
Pregnancy/Day by Day by Sheila Kitzinger and Vicky Bailey.
While Waiting by George E. Verrilli, MD, and Anne Marie Mueser.

The First Three Months

2

Your body changes very quickly during the first three months (each three months is called a **trimester**) of your pregnancy as it adapts to carrying a baby. You're likely to feel many of these changes, even though they are not usually visible to others. At the same time, your baby is growing from a single cell into an embryo that is beginning to move its limbs.

SOME OF THE QUESTIONS ANSWERED IN THIS CHAPTER INCLUDE:

- How is my baby growing?
- What can I do about "morning sickness?"
- Why do I have to go to the bathroom so often?
- What should I do for headaches?
- What are the signs of miscarriage?
- What kinds of tests will I have at the clinic?

How is my baby
growing?

YOUR BABY'S DEVELOPMENT

Your baby's life starts with just one egg in your body, joined with one sperm cell from the father. Less than an hour after these two cells have merged into one, they have begun to divide and multiply. First this looks simply like a cluster of cells, nothing like a baby. As the cells continue to multiply, they start to become specific parts of the human body.

A woman may not know yet that she's pregnant during the first month, but the baby is already growing rapidly. By the end of the first month, your baby's heart begins to beat and other organs are starting to develop. The baby is about 3/16 of an inch long, and there are dark spots where the eyes will later be.

During the second month the baby's brain and spinal cord are developing. The baby's head seems big, compared to the rest of the body. By the end of this month, the baby is about an inch long and weighs less than 1/10 of an ounce. Fingers and toes are just starting to develop.

The baby's length triples during the third month, up to about 3 inches. Now the baby weighs about an ounce. Fingers and toes are developed, and fingernails and toenails are beginning to form. There are even the beginnings of what will become the baby's teeth. The sex organs are now visible.

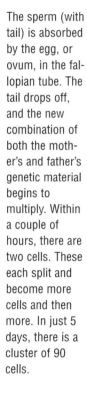

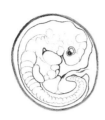

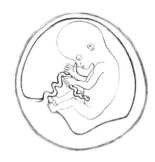

The sperm (with tail) is absorbed by the egg, or ovum, in the fallopian tube. The tail drops off, and the new combination of both the mother's and father's genetic material begins to multiply. Within a couple of hours, there are two cells. These each split and become more cells and then more. In just 5 days, there is a cluster of 90 cells.

At 4 weeks, the embryo is taking on shape, with a head and the beginning of what will be eyes.

At 8 weeks, the facial features are forming, and the baby has fingers and toes. In fact, the beginnings of all body parts and functions are now present. At 8 weeks, the embryo becomes a "fetus."

At 12 weeks, the baby's heart is complete, and the skeleton is beginning to form. The baby's proportions are close to what they will be at birth, with the head about 1/3 the size of the body.

WHAT'S HAPPENING TO YOUR BODY

YOUR BODY is changing a great deal, very quickly, during the first trimester, and it's natural for that to cause discomfort at times. Pay attention to the signals your body is sending—if you feel tired, for example, it's telling you to rest—and remember that you are likely to feel better during the second trimester.

Some of the physical changes you may experience include breast tenderness, nausea and vomiting, tiredness, faintness, frequent urination, headaches, and vaginal discharge.

BREAST TENDERNESS

For many women, sore and tender breasts are what tells them they are pregnant. Your breasts are preparing to feed a baby, so the milk glands are enlarging and the amount of fatty tissue is increasing. Your nipples may get darker and wider, and you may notice bluish veins under the skin on your breasts.

You may need to use a larger bra now, or one that is more supportive than what you've worn before. There are maternity bras, which have wide straps and backs, but any supportive bra may work for you. Cotton bras are best because they let your skin breathe.

NAUSEA AND VOMITING

If only it were just "morning sickness!" You can feel sick to your stomach anytime during the day or night, and some women say they are queasy nearly all the time during the first trimester of their pregnancy.

The good news is that this discomfort usually only occurs during the first trimester.

Some things that may help:

What can I do about "morning sickness?"

- *Keep crackers nearby and nibble a couple when you start to feel queasy, or before you get out of bed in the morning.*
- *Eat small meals several times a day so your stomach is never empty.*
- *Eat slowly.*
- *Eat a little lean meat or cheese before going to bed.*
- *Wait until after eating to drink fluids.*

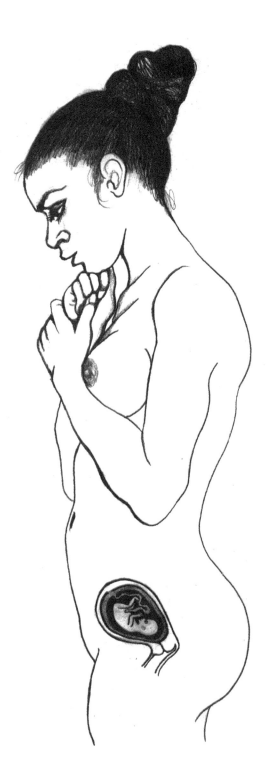

You may not "look pregnant" to others by the end of the third month, but your tummy is beginning to round as your uterus fills up more of your pelvic cavity. Your baby is about 4 inches long now.

- *Avoid foods that often trigger nausea for pregnant women, such as fried foods, spicy foods, seafood, citrus juices, or drinks with caffeine like coffee, tea, and cola.*
- *Avoid very hot or very cold temperatures in what you drink and in your home or office.*

If your nausea is severe or constant, talk to your health care provider about things that may help, including Vitamin B6 or wheat germ. Very few women have nausea so severe that they need hospital care.

Tiredness

It's normal to feel very tired during the first few months of your pregnancy. This tiredness is caused by the dramatic changes in your hormones during this time.

It may be hard, especially if you have a job or other children, but when you feel tired, you should try to rest. Go to bed earlier than you usually do and take naps whenever you can.

Regular exercise usually does not make you more tired—just the opposite. Exercise stimulates circulation and is good for you and the baby. Walking is particularly good, and it's usually easy to fit into your routine.

During your pregnancy, you may be more likely to develop **anemia**. When you are anemic, your blood does not carry oxygen to the rest of your body the way it should. Your tiredness may be at least partly caused by anemia. Talk to your health care provider about severe tiredness.

Faintness

During the first few months of your pregnancy you may suddenly feel dizzy or faint when you stand up after sitting or lying down. Or you may get faint after standing for a long time, especially in a warm room. This faintness may be caused by low blood pressure, low blood sugar, or anemia.

If you feel faint, sit and put your head down between your knees. Get up slowly, if you've been sitting or lying down. If you have to stand for a while, move around and exercise your legs.

Eating 5 or 6 small meals throughout the day can help keep up your blood sugar.

FREQUENT URINATION

As your uterus grows with the baby, it presses on your bladder and you need to go to the bathroom more often. Most women notice this most during the first few months and then again during the last few months.

You need to drink plenty of fluids—8 to 10 glasses (8 ounces per glass) or more each day—to stay healthy during your pregnancy, but you can drink most of it earlier in the day so you won't have to get up to go to the bathroom many times during the night.

Kegel exercises (see previous chapter) can strengthen your pelvic muscles to control your urine so you don't "dribble" at embarrassing moments.

Why do I have to go to the bathroom so often?

HEADACHES

When you feel a headache starting, lie down in a dark, quiet room if you can. A hot or cold compress (like a washcloth) at the back of your neck may help.

Most health care providers think that acetaminophen (Tylenol) is safe to take during pregnancy. Do not take aspirin or ibuprofen without first consulting with your health care provider.

Talk with your health care provider if your headaches are longer or stronger than usual, or your vision changes. This kind of headache is sometimes a sign of high blood pressure, and you and your baby may need special care.

What should I do for headaches?

VAGINAL DISCHARGE

Your vaginal discharge may change several times during your pregnancy. You may be more prone to yeast infections or other vaginal infections. Your health care provider can give you medication that will not harm your baby, to treat these infections. Do not douche during pregnancy, and do not use any suppositories, such as yeast medication, without talking to your health care provider.

MISCARRIAGE

MORE THAN 20 percent of all pregnancies end in miscarriage, usually during the first trimester. Often there's no apparent reason for a miscarriage, but probably it is because your body recognizes that something is not going well with the development of the baby or the pregnancy and begins a natural process to end the pregnancy.

Even though it is natural and common, miscarriage can be a very difficult loss for a woman and her partner. You've been looking forward to this baby, you've started to dream about what it will mean to be parents, you may have told your friends and relatives ... and now those lovely dreams are gone. You may feel guilt. Did I do something wrong? Can I get pregnant again? Will I lose another baby if I do?

Your health care provider can help give you answers to these questions that are specific to you and your pregnancy. It's very unlikely that you did anything to cause the miscarriage. Exercise, sex, strong emotions, or even a bad fall rarely cause miscarriage. Having a miscarriage, even if it's not your first, doesn't necessarily indicate anything about your ability to become pregnant again or to carry a baby to term.

SIGNS THAT YOU MAY BE HAVING A MISCARRIAGE

If you have any of the following signs, you should call your health care provider immediately. You may be told to stay home and watch your symptoms, or you may be told to come in right away.

- **Bleeding or spotting.** Pink or brown discharge, less than during a period. Spotting in the first months of pregnancy doesn't necessarily mean that you will have a miscarriage, but it's a symptom you should pay attention to.
- **Cramping.** Some cramping similar to what you feel during a menstrual period is normal, but cramping and bleeding together may signal a miscarriage.
- **Heavy bleeding.** Bright red blood, as heavy as a menstrual period or more.
- **Intense cramping.** You may feel continuous cramps, or very heavy ones that come and go. This is much more painful than the cramps you may have had with your period.
- **Passing of large clots.** A white or gray clot along with larger blood clots may mean you already have had a miscarriage. You should save the pregnancy tissue and show it to your health care provider.

What are the signs of miscarriage?

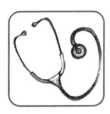

What kinds of tests will I have at the clinic?

CLINIC VISITS

YOUR FIRST VISIT will be longer and more involved, and you may want to have your partner with you so both of you can ask questions.

Your height, weight, and blood pressure will be taken. (Your weight and blood pressure will be taken on every visit to the clinic during your pregnancy.) Your health care providers will take a health history and ask you questions about diet, habits, and family medical history.

The health care provider will examine your ears, eyes, nose, throat, heart, lungs, breasts, abdomen, and lymph nodes. You will have a pelvic exam to check your vagina, cervix, uterus, fallopian tubes, and ovaries. The size of your uterus will be measured to help determine just how many weeks pregnant you are. If you are far enough along, your health care provider will listen for your baby's heartbeat. A Pap test will be done to screen for abnormalities or signs of cervical cancer.

You will be asked for samples of blood and urine so that laboratory tests can be done. Your blood type, Rh factor, and iron count will be checked. Your blood will be tested for certain sexually-transmitted diseases that can affect your baby, and for whether you have had German measles or have been exposed to hepatitis. You will also be offered an HIV test. Your urine will be checked for the levels of sugar and protein, and for any infection.

ULTRASOUND

An ultrasound may be given during your first or second trimester. It is not a routine test and will be done only if your health care provider feels it is medically necessary. The ultrasound uses high frequency sound waves to produce a picture of your baby.

The procedure is simple: You lie down and your abdomen is covered with a gel. Then the health care provider passes a transducer, or special microphone, over your abdomen. Usually you and the health care provider can watch the image on a screen as the transducer is moved. You may be given a "picture" of your baby to take with you.

Your health care provider may use the ultrasound to check:

- **The number of babies.**
- **The location of the placenta.**
- **The estimated due date.**
- **The baby's weight.**
- **The baby's growth and development.**

FOR PARTNERS

This is a good time to learn more about pregnancy. The two of you might even read some books together, so you both understand what she is going through. There's a lot both of you may not know, especially if this is a first pregnancy.

The more you share in the pregnancy, the better she is likely to feel. Go with her to the health care provider, at least for the first visit. (If you can, go every time.) Ask your own questions.

Do more around the house. She really is tired. Her body is doing a lot of work that you can't see, and she needs plenty of rest. A little pampering goes a long way toward having a healthier pregnancy and baby.

You may feel like this newly-pregnant person is not the woman you know. She's tired much of the time, she's running to the bathroom every 15 minutes, she's throwing up, she doesn't want to be touched....

The best thing you can do is be patient. Understand that this is all normal—and it doesn't last for very long.

If the pregnancy ends in a miscarriage, encourage her to talk about what it means to her—and be sure to talk about your own feelings as well. Most couples need some time to grieve this loss.

FOR MORE INFORMATION

Our Stories of Miscarriage by Rachel Faldet and Karen Fitton.
A Child is Born by Lennart Nilsson.
Active Birth by Janet Balaskas.
The Birth Partner by Penny Simkin.
Essential Exercises for the Childbearing Year by Elizabeth Noble.
Pregnancy, Childbirth and the Newborn by Penny Simkin and others.
Pregnancy/Day by Day by Sheila Kitzinger and Vicky Bailey.
While Waiting by George E. Verrilli, MD, and Anne Marie Mueser.

The Second Three Months

The fourth, fifth, and sixth months of pregnancy are often the "golden" time for many women. Any queasiness and tiredness you felt earlier are gone, you have more energy—and you're finally starting to *look* pregnant. You also begin to feel the movements of your developing baby.

SOME OF THE QUESTIONS ANSWERED IN THIS CHAPTER INCLUDE:

- How is my baby growing?
- What's happening to my body?
- Is it normal to feel blue?
- How do I prepare my other children for a new baby?
- What tests will my health care provider do?

How is my baby
growing?

YOUR BABY'S DEVELOPMENT

BY THE BEGINNING of the fourth month, your baby's heartbeat can be heard with a stethoscope. The brain looks like an adult's, but smaller. The baby is about 8½ inches long, weighs 6 ounces, and has eyebrows and eyelashes. Many babies begin to suck their thumbs about now.

During the fifth month, right around 20 weeks, you will begin to feel your baby's movements. This used to be called the "quickening," meaning that the baby had just come to life. Actually, your baby has been moving for quite a while but was too small for you to feel it before. Now the baby's twists and turns cause you to feel an odd, butterfly-like sensation in your abdomen. By the end of the fifth month, your baby weighs about a pound and is about 12 inches long.

A protective covering called **vernix** develops during the sixth month of pregnancy. This cream cheese-like material will stay on your baby right through birth, protecting his or her skin from drying. Your baby's skin is reddish and wrinkled now. The baby's eyes are open and sensitive to light. The ears are developed, and your baby can hear sounds. It's a good time to have conversations, even to sing, to the baby inside you.

Your baby is already an individual, with unique fingerprints and footprints, by the end of the sixth month. He or she is about 14 inches long and weighs about 2 pounds.

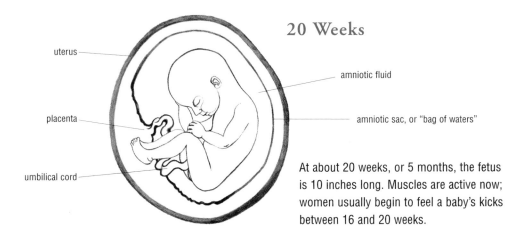

20 Weeks

uterus

amniotic fluid

placenta

amniotic sac, or "bag of waters"

umbilical cord

At about 20 weeks, or 5 months, the fetus is 10 inches long. Muscles are active now; women usually begin to feel a baby's kicks between 16 and 20 weeks.

What's Happening to Your Body

FINALLY, you look pregnant. Your breasts are large (although they may not have grown any more since the first couple of months), and your belly is rounded. Most women begin wearing maternity clothing sometime during the second trimester of their pregnancy.

Whether you wear maternity clothing or not, make sure that you choose clothing that is comfortable and that doesn't bind you.

Physically, the second trimester of pregnancy often is a "golden" time. The nausea of early pregnancy usually ends before or during the fourth month and all of a sudden you are *hungry*. The fatigue caused by your hormonal adjustment is gone, and you may feel very energetic.

Keep healthy food around to satisfy your hunger—fruit and raw vegetables, not salty snacks. Eating a balanced diet may have been difficult during the first trimester, when you were often queasy. Now is a good time to make sure you're eating well.

Some physical changes you may experience during the second trimester of your pregnancy include:

Heartburn

As your baby grows, your stomach gets squeezed and stomach acid may back up the esophagus, causing a burning sensation in your upper abdomen. Eating frequent small meals, rather than large ones, helps. Don't lie down right after eating, and sleep with your head propped up, to keep the stomach acid from backing up. Talk to your health care provider about antacids if changes in your diet don't help.

Constipation

Hormones make your digestive system work more slowly, and constipation is a common problem during pregnancy. You can ease constipation by drinking lots of fluids, eating high fiber foods, such as bran, raisins, and raw vegetables and fruit, and getting regular daily exercise.

What's happening to
my body?

12 to 16 Weeks   16 to 20 Weeks   20 to 24 Weeks

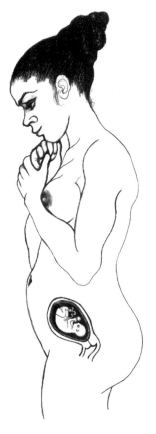

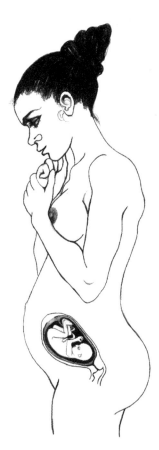

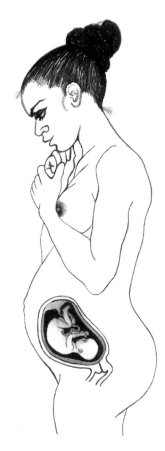

By 4 months, you probably have gained about nine pounds. Less than 2 pounds of that is the baby, the placenta, and the amniotic fluid; the rest is accounted for by the increased blood volume and fat tissue that prepares you to nurse your baby.

Around 20 weeks, your uterus is about level with your navel, and your abdomen is swelling. If others haven't noticed you were pregnant before, they are likely to now.

The skin on your abdomen is stretching as your baby grows, and you may see red streaks, or stretch marks, on your belly. If your skin is light, these marks will fade to a silver color after your baby is born. If you have dark skin, the marks will stay dark.

SKIN CHANGES

Changing hormones may change your skin. You may develop blemishes—or those blemishes you have may clear up. Some women get a darkening of the skin on their face or abdomen. Dry, itchy skin is common. A good skin care routine will help some of these problems. Clean your skin with a mild soap (don't use deodorant soap) and warm—not hot—water. Then follow with a good moisturizer. One that is unscented is less likely to cause itching. Remember that these skin problems will go away after the baby is born.

ROUND LIGAMENT PAIN

The ligaments that help support the uterus are stretching as your baby grows, and sometimes that can cause a sharp pain on either or both sides of the uterus. You are likely to feel this pain when you make quick movements or you cough or sneeze. This pain is common about the fifth month of pregnancy, but can also happen later. If you feel a pain, bend toward the side that hurts or pull your knee toward your chest. A warm pack or hot water bottle on the area also may help.

PREPARING FOR BREASTFEEDING

IF YOU THINK you would like to breastfeed your baby, you can begin preparing your breasts now to help make your early breast-feeding experiences pleasant and comfortable.

The best preparation for breastfeeding is to eat a well-balanced, healthy diet, to get enough sleep, and to learn how to relax. Your body will do the rest.

You should:

Keep your breasts clean, but wash only with warm water.

Your nipples have special glands that make a substance that helps keep your nipples soft and protects against infection. You don't want to wash it off with soap.

Support your breasts with a good bra.

If you normally are small-breasted, you may need to purchase a bra that gives you more support. This doesn't mean lots of wires or uncomfortable ribbing, but something made from natural fibers—like cotton—with wide straps.

EMOTIONS

THE SECOND TRIMESTER of pregnancy is a time when you are likely to feel focused outward. You are beginning to look rounder, so others may comment on your pregnancy, giving you advice and congratulations. You have more energy, so you are likely to be doing more than during the first trimester. It can be a very happy time.

Is it normal to feel blue?

As you start to feel your baby move, the fact that your life is going to change with this new baby becomes very real. Some days that may feel wonderful; on other days it may feel frightening. It's normal to have the blues sometimes, even when everything is going well.

It's important to talk about your concerns with others—your partner, friends, family, and health care providers. If you don't have support, your health care providers can refer you to agencies and services that may help.

YOUR OTHER CHILDREN

YOU MAY HAVE waited to talk about the new baby coming, but now you're starting to look different and other adults are talking about the baby. It's usually a good time to share the news with your other children.

Emphasize the positive—"You're going to be a brother or sister"—rather than what they may see as an intrusion—"You're going to have a new brother or sister." Remind them, every day, that you love them by telling them, by hugging and cuddling, by giving them your attention.

The following are some ways to help your children accept the idea of a new baby:

- *Talk about the baby with them. Let them feel the baby's movements.*
- *If you're going to make major changes, like putting them in a different bedroom, don't do it right before the birth.*
- *Read books about new babies with your children.*
- *Show them pictures of themselves when they were first born, and talk about that time.*
- *Take them for tours of the birthing area, so they will know where they can visit you.*

How do I prepare my other children for a new baby?

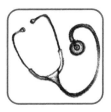

What tests will my health care provider recommend?

CLINIC VISITS

YOU PROBABLY will see your health care provider about once a month during this part of your pregnancy.

Your weight, blood pressure, and urine will be sampled during each visit. The health care provider will listen to the baby's heart, measure the baby's growth, and ask you about the baby's movements. Some special tests may be recommended during this period. These include:

TRIPLE SCREEN TEST

This blood test is done to screen for Down Syndrome and for abnormalities in the spinal cord. The test can be done at anytime between 15 and 21 weeks into the pregnancy, but the best time is 16 weeks.

The triple screen is not a required test, but it is offered to everyone. It's really a combination of three tests: alpha-fetoprotein (AFP), unconjugated serum estriol, and human chorionic gonadotropin (HCG). The AFP can indicate possible spinal cord abnormalities; all three tests are needed to determine the risk for Down Syndrome.

The triple screen test predicts the risk of abnormality, not whether your baby actually has an abnormality. If the risk is high, other tests will be offered to diagnose any problem.

ULTRASOUND

What is an ultrasound?

An **ultrasound** may be given during your first or second trimester. It is not a routine test and will be done only if your health care provider feels it is medically necessary. The ultrasound uses high frequency sound waves to produce a picture of your baby. (See page 31 for more discussion of an ultrasound test.)

AMNIOCENTESIS

This test is used to diagnose certain genetic disorders or, later in pregnancy, to check on other aspects of the baby's health.

A local anesthetic, like Novocain, is used to numb the skin on your abdomen. A thin needle is then inserted through your abdomen and a small amount of amniotic fluid is withdrawn to be tested in a lab. There is a risk to the baby with this test, which is only done if medically necessary. Your health care provider will discuss the procedure and its risks with you, if amniocentesis is suggested.

CHILDBIRTH CLASSES

IT'S TIME to look into the variety of childbirth preparation classes and to sign up. The staff at your clinic can refer you to the classes that are right for you.

FOR PARTNERS

ENJOY this "golden" period of the pregnancy with your partner, but remember that she still needs a little extra care. It's a good time for both of you to do some of the planning for the arrival of the new family member. You might decorate the baby's room, get some of the equipment you will need (a car seat, a crib, a stroller), and start investigating for daycare.

One of the best things you can do for your partner now is to support and encourage her in developing a healthy lifestyle. Take walks with her, plan healthy meals, go grocery shopping and help select healthy snacks rather than fatty, non-nutritive ones. It will be good for both of you.

If there are already children in the home, help reassure them that they are loved. Encourage them to talk about the baby. Listen to their fears and concerns about the baby.

Sign up for and make plans to attend childbirth classes with her. And in the meantime, attend as many clinic visits with her as you can.

FOR MORE INFORMATION

A Child is Born by Lennart Nilsson.
Active Birth by Janet Balaskas.
The Birth Partner by Penny Simkin.
Essential Exercises for the Childbearing Year by Elizabeth Noble.
Pregnancy, Childbirth and the Newborn by Penny Simkin and others.
Pregnancy/Day by Day by Sheila Kitzinger and Vicky Bailey.
While Waiting by George E. Verrilli, MD, and Anne Marie Mueser.

The Final Three Months

You're getting bigger—you may think you're *huge*—and you can't wait for this baby to arrive. At the same time, you may be nervous and even a little sad about the end of this stage of your life. There are lots of things to do before the baby arrives, so this is a very busy time for you.

SOME OF THE QUESTIONS ANSWERED IN THIS CHAPTER INCLUDE:

- How is my baby growing?
- Is it normal for my feet to swell like this?
- What do I do to get ready for the baby?
- What if I'm placing my baby for adoption?
- How often will I see my health care provider?

YOUR BABY'S DEVELOPMENT

DURING THE LAST trimester of pregnancy, your baby is growing and getting stronger. Although the baby's organs and systems are developed, they need these final weeks to mature before a healthy birth. A premature baby born at the end of the seventh month may live, but one born at the end of the eighth month is even more likely to live.

By the end of the eighth month, your baby may weigh as much as 5 pounds and be 18 inches long. At the end of the ninth month, an average full-term baby weighs about 7½ pounds. Yours may be even heavier.

You may feel your baby hiccuping during the last 8 to 10 weeks of pregnancy, as well as kicking and pushing heavily against your abdomen.

During the ninth month, the baby's head drops into your pelvis as the preparation for birth begins.

How is my baby growing?

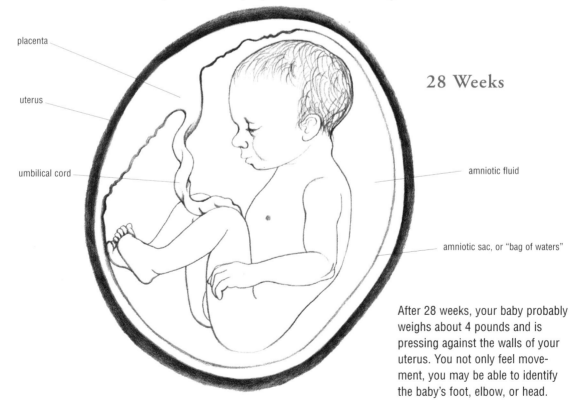

placenta

uterus

umbilical cord

28 Weeks

amniotic fluid

amniotic sac, or "bag of waters"

After 28 weeks, your baby probably weighs about 4 pounds and is pressing against the walls of your uterus. You not only feel movement, you may be able to identify the baby's foot, elbow, or head.

WHAT'S HAPPENING TO YOUR BODY

JUST GETTING UP out of a chair may feel like a big deal during the last month or two of your pregnancy. Your baby is getting big, and you may feel awkward. Sleeping may be harder because you can't find a comfortable position. Your feet get tired. As the baby drops into birth position, your bladder is squeezed and you have to go to the bathroom more frequently.

Most of the physical difficulties in the last trimester of pregnancy are the result of the increasing size of the baby—and you. Some things you may experience include:

BACKACHE

You tend to walk, stand, and sit differently when you're pregnant, and this can strain the muscles in your back. Sometimes the baby's head may press against your spine, causing a lower backache. Try to keep your shoulder straight, and avoid wearing high heels.

FREQUENT URINATION

The baby's position changes in late pregnancy and puts pressure on your bladder, so you will need to urinate more frequently. Don't hold your urine; this can cause a bladder infection. Keep drinking plenty of fluids, and try to empty your bladder fully whenever you urinate.

CONTRACTIONS

The muscles of your uterus tighten and relax frequently during your pregnancy, although you usually can't feel the contractions until the fourth month or later. Sometimes referred to as **Braxton-Hicks contractions**, these irregular contractions do not get stronger and are not signs of labor. You can continue your normal activities, especially walking. (For more information on early contractions, see the section on preterm labor beginning on page 51.)

VARICOSE VEINS

Your slower circulation and the pressure of your growing baby can cause **varicose veins**, usually later in pregnancy. Avoid standing for long periods, do not sit with your legs or ankles crossed, and try to rest a few times each day with your legs up. Your health care provider may recommend elastic stockings.

24 to 28 Weeks   28 to 32 Weeks   32 to 36 Weeks

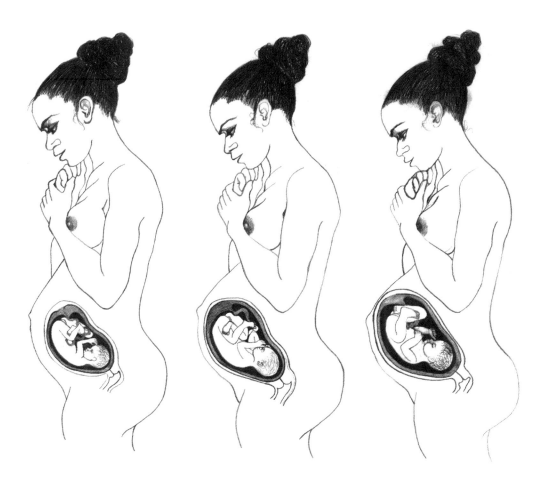

During these last months, your baby may nearly double in weight. You are heavier, not just from the baby, but from an increase in body fat and blood volume. The baby's head presses against your bladder, which causes you to go to the bathroom more often, and the baby's bottom presses against your diaphragm, making you short of breath.

HEMORRHOIDS

Your baby's growth, and the increase in your blood supply during pregnancy, put pressure on the veins in your rectum. Many women develop hemorrhoids. You can help avoid them by eating foods that will keep you from getting constipated. Kegel exercises (see page 11), which strengthen the muscles of your anus as well as your vagina, may also help. If you do get hemorrhoids, an ice pack, a tub bath, or a cloth soaked with cold witch hazel can help you feel better. Avoid sleeping on your back, which can aggravate hemorrhoids. Ask your health care giver about medications that might help.

LEG CRAMPS

Leg cramps usually happen while you're in bed. Your body doesn't absorb calcium as well when you're pregnant, and this lack of calcium can cause muscle cramps. Eating and drinking foods with calcium—dark green leafy vegetables, dried fruits, nuts, beans, and dairy products like milk, cheese, and yogurt—can help prevent leg cramps. If you get a cramp, stay calm and then pull your toes back toward you and push your heel away. This stretches the muscles and releases the cramp.

SWELLING

Some women find that their shoes no longer fit. Swelling in your feet, ankles, and legs is normal during pregnancy. As your uterus gets bigger, there is pressure on the blood vessels in your legs. Try to avoid standing for a long time, and when you sit or lie down, put your feet up and don't cross your legs. Wear loose clothing that doesn't bind anywhere. Drinking lots of fluids will not increase the swelling, but will actually help reduce it by keeping your kidneys working well. If you see a big change in the amount of swelling you have—including in your face and hands—or if you have a sudden weight gain, call your health care provider right away.

Is it normal for my feet to swell like this?

LEAKING BREASTS

Your breasts are getting ready to feed a baby, and may leak a yellowish or clear liquid called **colostrum** toward the end of your pregnancy. This is normal but can be embarrassing. A cotton cloth or pad in your bra will absorb the leaks. Wash the dried liquid from your nipples with plain warm water, not soap.

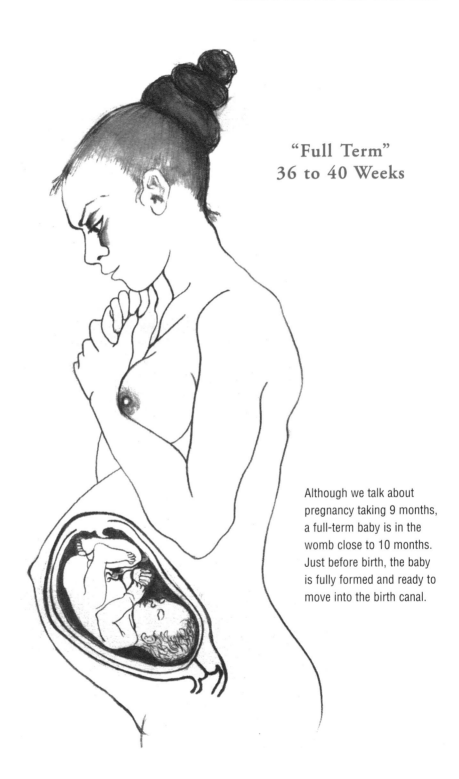

"Full Term" 36 to 40 Weeks

Although we talk about pregnancy taking 9 months, a full-term baby is in the womb close to 10 months. Just before birth, the baby is fully formed and ready to move into the birth canal.

GETTING READY FOR BABY

THERE MAY BE a lot to do before your baby arrives. You will want to have a place for your baby to sleep, blankets, diapers, clothing, a car seat, a stroller … the list can seem very long.

Childbirth classes are recommended during the last trimester. You and your partner—or whoever will be your labor coach—will learn what to expect when your baby is born, and you'll meet other people who are going through the same thing. Classes remind you that there are still decisions to be made, such as:

- **If my baby is a boy, should he be circumcised?**
- **Should I breastfeed?**
- **If I'm going back to work soon after my baby is born, who will I find for daycare?**

This is a good time to get information about these choices. Ask your health care provider about circumcision, and do some reading as well. Your health care provider may direct you to a breastfeeding specialist (called a lactation consultant) or classes, so you can feel more comfortable about breastfeeding even before your baby is born. Tour daycare centers now, or visit the home where you will leave your baby while you work. Get a sense of what kind of care is given to the other children and see if that feels all right to you.

If you haven't selected a health care provider for your baby yet, now is the time, so that he or she can begin taking care of your baby in the hospital.

Being prepared can help you feel more relaxed. Freeze some extra meals so you won't have to worry about cooking when you come home with a new baby. Stock up on supplies for yourself, such as maxipads, nursing bras, compresses that can be heated or chilled, and supplies for your baby.

If you're planning to use disposable diapers, expect to use 8 to 10 diapers a day, and have at least a week's worth of the smaller-sized disposables ready for your newborn.

If you're going to use cloth diapers and wash them yourself, think about how often you want to wash diapers. About 4 dozen

What do I do to get ready for the baby?

will keep you from having to wash diapers every day in order to have a good supply of clean ones. If you are using a diaper service, the service will provide you with the necessary amount.

For your baby's first clothes, get simple, inexpensive shirts, nightgowns, and infant suits. You will be surprised at how quickly your baby will outgrow the first clothes. You probably will change your baby's clothes 2 or 3 times a day, so you may want to have enough clothes that you will not need to wash every day.

Showers, garage sales, and hand-me-downs are good ways to get the supplies you need. Be sure, however, that any used equipment meets federal safety standards.

You will need a federally-approved infant car seat as soon as your baby is born if you are planning to take him or her home from the hospital in a car.

ADOPTION

IF YOU ARE placing your baby for adoption, it is important to have a general plan in place so that your hospital stay will be easier. If you have not done so already, the beginning of the last trimester of your pregnancy is when you should work with a social agency or lawyer to learn about your options for placing your baby with a family.

Some questions to consider include:

- **How much contact do you want to have with the baby during your hospital stay?**
- **What kind of family will you want to care for your baby?**
- **What feelings do you have about placing your baby in another family's care?**
- **How will you say good-bye to your baby? Or will you continue to have contact?**

Talk with your health care providers about your adoption plans so they can support you in the last months of pregnancy, both in the hospital and during the first weeks at home. This may be a difficult time for you. Talking about your feelings and decisions with others can help.

What if I'm placing my baby for adoption?

PRETERM LABOR

LABOR is considered "preterm" if it occurs more than 3 weeks before your due date—or before 37 weeks of pregnancy. Not all preterm labor means a premature birth. Often labor can be stopped, and the baby can be given more time to develop and grow before birth.

What if my baby is born prematurely?

If you have vaginal bleeding or fluid leaking from the vagina, you should call your health care provider immediately. Other symptoms of preterm labor are sometimes hard to recognize because they are like normal discomforts of pregnancy. Often the only difference is how strong the symptom is, how regularly it occurs, or how long it lasts. Be aware of these signs of possible preterm labor:

- **Change in vaginal discharge**
  If the discharge is watery or bloody, call your health care provider immediately.
- **Increased pelvic pressure, for an hour**
  This is a very heavy feeling, as if your baby is pushing down, in your back, thighs, and lower abdomen.
- **Cramps, like menstrual cramps, for an hour**
- **Dull backache below the waistline, for an hour**
  Most women have some backache during pregnancy. A low backache that comes and goes but doesn't go away when you change position may be a sign of preterm labor.
- **Five or more contractions or feelings of tightening in an hour**
- **Intestinal cramps, for an hour**
  There may be diarrhea, but not necessarily.
- **"Something doesn't feel right" or "something feels different"**
  Trust your instincts and call your health care provider.

If you have any of these symptoms, empty your bladder, drink a glass of water, lie down on your side for an hour, and feel for contractions or other symptoms. Time the contractions. If you have had 5 or 6 during the hour, or you still have other symptoms, call your health care provider.

HOW TO HELP PREVENT A PRETERM BIRTH

- *Drink 8 to 10 glasses of liquid every day.* Water, milk, and juices are best. Don't drink more than 2 or 3 caffeinated drinks like coffee or cola a day.
- *Prevent and treat constipation.*
- *Empty your bladder frequently.*
- *Decrease stress in your life.*
- *Avoid strenuous activities if they cause contractions.*
- *Stop smoking.*
- *Do NOT prepare your nipples for breastfeeding.* (Some books recommend this, but the stimulation can bring on early labor).
- *Report signs of a bladder infection to your health care provider.*
- *Eat regular, nutritious meals.*
- *Be aware of contractions and warning signs.*
  If you notice tightening or other symptoms, do the following for 30 minutes:
  - *Lie on your left side with a pillow behind your back for support.*
  - *Place your fingertips on your abdomen.*
  - *If your uterus feels tight and hard, like a clenched fist, and then gets soft again, you are having a contraction.*
  - *Keep track of the time from one contraction starting to the next one starting.* (See page 67 for information on how to time your contractions.)

It's normal to have some contractions during pregnancy, but more than 5 or 6 in an hour is too many, and you should call your health care provider.

If you are at risk for preterm labor, your health care provider may give you more specific instructions.

CLINIC VISITS

AROUND YOUR eighth month of pregnancy, you will begin seeing your health care provider every other week. During the last month, these visits will be every week. Partners are encouraged to attend these visits, too.

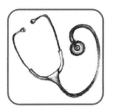

How often will I see my health care provider?

The usual weight and blood pressure measurements will be taken, and your urine and blood will be checked. Your health care provider will listen to your baby's heartbeat and measure the baby's growth.

If your blood is Rh-negative, at about the beginning of the seventh month of pregnancy, or 28 weeks, your health care provider will recommend that you have an injection of RhoGAM. This will prevent your body building up antibodies against your baby, in case your baby's blood is Rh-positive.

Pelvic examinations by your health care provider during the last month or so of your pregnancy can help determine when your baby will be born. As you approach the baby's due date, the cervix gets thinner and begins to open. This is called effacement (thinning) and dilation (opening). You may hear your health care provider say things like "You're 30 percent effaced," or "dilation is one centimeter."

GESTATIONAL DIABETES SCREENING

Gestational diabetes occurs in up to 12 percent of all pregnancies in the United States and can be a concern for the health of both the mother and the baby. If it's diagnosed early, complications during the pregnancy can be prevented.

Before your visit, the clinic nurse will give you instructions about the test, which is usually done at 28 weeks. At the clinic, you will be given a sugar solution to drink and then, an hour later, a blood sample will be taken. The results are often ready immediately. If the blood sugar results are high, further testing may be done.

FOR PARTNERS

GETTING READY for the baby is something the two of you can do together. Paint a bedroom, look for a crib, gather the supplies you will need when the baby arrives.

It can be fun to cook together, preparing meals that you can freeze and use during the first weeks after the baby is born. You are likely to find yourself very busy when the baby arrives, just like your partner. She'll need a certain amount of tending—and so will the baby. Even if you're a wonderful cook, you may find yourself out of time, and those prepared meals will come in handy.

Ask your partner what special things you can do for her: perhaps rubbing her back, shopping for groceries, or bathing the other children.

Learn everything you can at childbirth classes, and make sure that both of you practice the breathing and relaxation exercises you are taught. There's a temptation to think you don't have to practice, that it will all come naturally, but it will be much better for both of you if you know what you're doing.

Visit the place your baby will be born with your partner. Find out what you should bring to make it more comfortable for labor and birth.

FOR MORE INFORMATION

Born Early by Lida Lafferty and Bo Flood.
A Child is Born by Lennart Nilsson.
Active Birth by Janet Balaskas.
The Birth Partner by Penny Simkin.
Essential Exercises for the Childbearing Year by Elizabeth Noble.
Pregnancy, Childbirth and the Newborn by Penny Simkin and others.
Pregnancy/Day by Day by Sheila Kitzinger and Vicky Bailey.
While Waiting by George E. Verrilli, MD, and Anne Marie Mueser.

Keeping Track of Your Pregnancy

The following pages are a place for you to write down thoughts, events, and changes during your pregnancy. Some of the pages can be used to help you and your health care provider work together; others let you remember your hopes and dreams about your baby.

YOU AND YOUR HEALTH CARE PROVIDER
QUESTIONS YOU HAVE ABOUT THIS PREGNANCY

When you think of things you want to remember to ask your health care provider, write them here. Take this book with you to each prenatal exam.

WHAT YOU'RE FEELING

It helps your health care provider if you keep track of what is happening to your body. Use this space to jot down anything that you think you might need to talk about. Are you feeling nauseated? When? Any unusual aches and pains? Trouble sleeping—or do you sleep all the time?

CLINIC VISITS

Use this space to record each visit to your health care provider.

Date of visit: _____ Weight: _____

Tests done: _____

Comments by health care provider: _____

_____

_____

Date of visit: _____ Weight: _____

Tests done: _____

Comments by health care provider: _____

_____

_____

Date of visit: _____ Weight: _____

Tests done: _____

Comments by health care provider: _____

_____

_____

Date of visit: _____ Weight: _____

Tests done: _____

Comments by health care provider: _____

_____

_____

Date of visit: _____ Weight: _____

Tests done: _____

Comments by health care provider: _____

_____

_____

Date of visit: _____ Weight: _____

Tests done: _____

Comments by health care provider: _____

_____

_____

Date of visit: Weight:

Tests done:

Comments by health care provider:

Date of visit: Weight:

Tests done:

Comments by health care provider:

Date of visit: Weight:

Tests done:

Comments by health care provider:

Date of visit: Weight:

Tests done:

Comments by health care provider:

Date of visit: Weight:

Tests done:

Comments by health care provider:

Date of visit: Weight:

Tests done:

Comments by health care provider:

BABY'S MOVEMENTS

WHEN DID you first feel your baby move? What did it make you feel? What were you thinking about?

_____

_____

_____

When do you most feel your baby moving? At what time of day or night? What are you likely to be doing?

_____

_____

_____

How does your baby respond to:
> your voice? (try talking to your baby, then singing.)

_____

> different kinds of music? (try listening to rock music, classical music, country music, rhythm and blues, etc.)

_____

> your movements?

_____

Can you tell the difference between your baby's foot and your baby's elbow? When could you start to feel this difference? Does your baby hiccup? When? For how long at a time?

_____

_____

_____

_____

HOPES AND DREAMS

WHAT KIND of home do you want to bring your baby into? What can you do to prepare for that?

_____

_____

_____

_____

_____

_____

_____

What are the most important things you can do for your baby?

_____

_____

_____

_____

_____

_____

_____

If you could wave a magic wand over your baby, what would you wish for?

_____

_____

_____

_____

_____

_____

_____

PLANNING THE BIRTH

WHO DO YOU want to be present at the birth of your baby?

Do you want medication to be offered? Would you rather not have medication offered unless you ask for it?

What position(s) would you like to use to give birth?

What would you like your health care providers to know about you?

During labor, how can your health care providers make you feel more comfortable?

---

more in control?

What items do you want to have with you during labor? (a special photograph? a tape player and favorite tape?)

Who would you like to cut the baby's umbilical cord?

Other plans?

Labor: Expectations

BEFORE YOUR baby is born, write your ideas about what going into labor and giving birth might be like.

How will your breathing and relaxation exercises help?

_____

_____

Will your baby come before, on, or after the due date?

_____

How will you go into labor? Will your water break or will you start having contractions?

_____

_____

How long will you be in labor?

_____

What medications, if any, do you think you may need?

_____

How difficult will labor be?

_____

_____

What will the urge to push feel like?

_____

_____

Will you have an episiotomy?

_____

What do you expect to feel just after your baby is born?

_____

_____

_____

LABOR: REALITY

AFTER YOUR BABY is born, write what actually happened and see how it compares with what you expected.

How did your breathing and relaxation exercises help?

_____

_____

Did your baby come before, on, or after the due date?

_____

How did you go into labor? Did your water break or did you start having contractions?

_____

_____

_____

How long were you in labor?

_____

What medications, if any, did you need?

_____

_____

How difficult was labor?

_____

_____

Did you have an episiotomy?

_____

What did you feel just after your baby was born?

_____

_____

_____

_____

_____

_____

Your Baby Arrives

Giving birth can take days, or just a couple of hours. Every woman's experience is different. And if you've had more than one baby, you know that even for the same woman, each birth is different. With the help of your health care providers, support persons, and partner, you can go into childbirth and labor feeling confident.

SOME OF THE QUESTIONS ANSWERED IN THIS CHAPTER INCLUDE:

- How will I know if I'm in labor?
- What do "dilation" and "effacement" mean?
- What happens during the transition phase?
- What is the afterbirth?
- What happens with a C-section?
- What kind of exercise can I do after having a baby?
- What if I don't love my baby right away?
- Why do I feel sad?

BEFORE LABOR

EVERY LABOR and birth is different, but there are some conditions that may indicate a baby is ready to be born. Any or all of the following may occur before the start of labor.

How will I know if I'm in labor?

- **Lightening or engagement.** The baby drops deeper into your pelvis, usually about 2 to 4 weeks before delivery. You will notice that you are able to breathe more easily and you'll have less heartburn, but you will have more lower back pain and you may find yourself making more trips to the bathroom.
- **Diarrhea or loose, frequent stools.**
- **Burst of energy.** Women call this the nesting instinct. Suddenly you're cleaning house, getting the baby's room ready, or cooking up a storm. Enjoy this burst of energy, but don't overdo it and tire yourself too much.
- **Large increase in vaginal discharge.** Discharge or mucus, called a **mucus plug**, may be pink or brownish. This discharge may be seen as long as 3 weeks before labor begins—or on the same day.
- **Low backache.** Use the pelvic rock exercise (see page 12) to stretch out your back. Warm baths, hot water bottles, or back rubs also help.
- **Softening of the cervix.** Your health care provider will notice this during a vaginal exam.
- **Rupture of "bag of waters."** Amniotic fluid may either leak or gush out. It's usually clear and odorless, and you may mistake it for urine at first. You should call your health care provider immediately if your water breaks. Note the time you noticed the liquid, the amount, and the color (clear, brown, yellow, green, or pinkish?) to tell your health care provider.
- **Contractions begin.** Regular contractions that get longer and stronger as time passes are an important sign that labor has begun.
- **Cervical effacement and dilation.** The most reliable sign that labor is under way is the thinning and opening of your cervix. This can be seen only in a cervical exam.

CONTRACTIONS

A contraction sometimes feels as if your lower abdomen has become a tight fist. (Bend your arm and "make a muscle" on your upper arm. Feel this muscle. This is what a contraction in your abdomen will feel like if you put your hand on it.) The contraction will loosen, then tighten a few minutes later. You may feel a dull ache in your back, coming all the way around to the front of your abdomen and down your thighs. In early labor, contractions usually feel like strong menstrual cramps.

Contractions are caused by the muscles at the top of your uterus tightening and pulling up the lower part of your uterus, making the cervix open, and then pressing the baby down through the cervix.

TIMING CONTRACTIONS

You will need to time your contractions. This means keeping track of how long they last and how often they happen.

Duration, or how long a contraction lasts, is timed from the beginning of a contraction to the end of that same contraction. It's usually measured in seconds.

Frequency, or how often contractions occur, is timed from the *beginning* of one contraction to the *beginning* of the next contraction. It's measured in minutes.

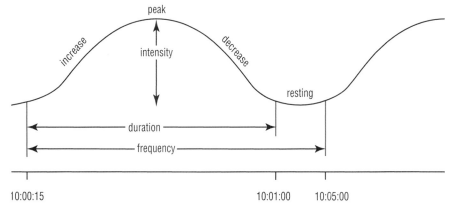

The duration, or length, of the contraction charted above is 45 seconds. The frequency, or time between the beginning of this contraction and the beginning of the next contraction, is 4 minutes and 45 seconds.

PRE-LABOR

You may feel contractions but not be in labor yet. This **false labor** is actually the body getting ready for birth, so it's more accurately called **pre-labor**. In true labor, the time between contractions will gradually shorten, and the contractions themselves will strengthen. You may start out feeling contractions every 15 minutes; then after an hour you will realize they are coming every 10 minutes, and it takes more concentration for you to breathe through them. Some women may start true labor with contractions that are strong right away and that come every 3 to 4 minutes.

Contractions in pre-labor don't come regularly, and are not likely to vary in strength. They may even weaken after a while.

Walking is a good way to test whether you are in true labor. If your contractions get stronger as you walk around, you are most likely in true labor. If they go away, or seem weaker as you walk, you are probably in pre-labor. Talking also helps test whether you are in true labor. If you can't talk while having contractions, it's likely to be true labor.

If you are still unsure, call your health care provider.

IF YOU THINK YOU ARE IN LABOR

If you think you are in labor, your health care provider will want to talk to you about whether you should come to the hospital. The tone of your voice gives your health care provider important information about your labor.

Questions your health care provider may ask include:

- **Has your water broken?**
- **Have you had a mucus plug?**
- **How regular and close together and are your contractions?**
- **When did your contractions start? When did they become regular?**
- **How are you feeling?**

WHEN TO CALL YOUR HEALTH CARE PROVIDER

If your "bag of waters" ruptures.

    Your health care provider may tell you to come to the hospital right away. Note the time that you noticed the rupture, and the amount and color of the fluid.

If you are having regular contractions and are uncomfortable.

    You or your partner should use a watch to time when one contraction starts and ends, and then when the next one starts and ends. Write down these times. Almost the first question your health care provider will ask is: "How frequent are your contractions?" Usually you will be told to come to the hospital when you have contractions that are 2 to 5 minutes apart and last at least 60 seconds. If this is not your first baby, you may be asked to come to the hospital even if your contractions are shorter in duration and frequency because your labor is likely to go more quickly.

If you don't feel safe or comfortable at home anymore.

If your health care provider gives you other guidelines about when to call, be sure to follow those, rather than the general guidelines listed here.

BREATHING AND RELAXATION

LEARNING HOW to breathe and relax properly can make your labor a much easier experience. Childbirth classes are an excellent place to learn and practice breathing and relaxation, even if this isn't your first baby. Even if you haven't taken childbirth classes, you can still use breathing and relaxation techniques—and the nurses helping you will be able to support you.

If you want to have a labor and delivery without pain medication, you must practice your breathing and relaxation with your partner or support person on a regular basis. Even if you plan on using pain medications, proper breathing and relaxation techniques will help you before you are given medication, or if the medication doesn't help as much as you expected.

BREATHING BASICS

Breathing gives you and your baby oxygen. Proper breathing during labor helps the uterus work more effectively and the cervix open more easily.

Remember to keep breathing.

It's a normal reaction to hold your breath if you feel pain, but breathing through the discomfort will help.

Finding a focal point, something to look at and concentrate on, may be helpful.

This focal point might be nothing more than a spot on the wall; but some women use a favorite photo or small item that they bring to the hospital with them. Other women prefer to look inward to concentrate.

Use a cleansing breath before and after each contraction.

"Cleansing breath" simply means inhaling deeply and exhaling slowly.

Try to relax between contractions.

You may change the pace and style of your breathing to help you cope in labor. Listen to what your body is telling you, and the nurses and health care provider will assist and support you.

Some breathing techniques that women have used in labor include:

- **Slow-paced breathing.** This is like an extension of the cleansing breath, from deep in your chest. Just take easy, deep breaths and release them slowly.
- **Steady-paced breathing.** These are shallower breaths from your chest. Say the word "hee" in order to keep your breaths coming at an even pace.
- **Varied-paced breathing.** This is more shallow breathing. You can time these breaths—especially with a birth partner's help—by counting a series of "hee's" ending with a puff. For example: "hee, hee, hee, blow."

  You can make yourself concentrate more on your breathing by varying the pattern: "hee, hee, hee, blow—hee, hee, blow—hee, blow—hee, hee, hee, blow," etc.
- **Breathing with the pushing urge.** You may have an overwhelming urge to push, even before it's time for the baby to be born. This urge may feel as if you need to move your bowels. Pushing often against a cervix that isn't fully open can cause the cervix to swell. To control this urge, you can keep repeating any word, pant like a dog, or make short bursts of air as if you're trying to blow hair off your forehead.

Illustrated below are some positions you may want to try when you are in labor—or when you just need to relax. Remember to use a variety of positions and to change positions frequently.

Positions for relaxation or labor

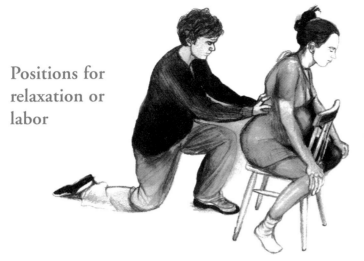

If you sit backwards on a chair, another person can rub your back and give you counter-pressure—that is, firm pressure against the lower back during a contraction. Counter-pressure can be especially helpful if you are feeling strong contractions against your lower back.

The side-lying position, with pillows to support your head and leg, can help you relax comfortably during contractions.

Getting on your hands and knees can help with labor pains in your lower back. It helps relieve the pressure of the baby's head on your tailbone. When you are in this position, another person can rub your back or give you counter-pressure. This position also may allow the baby to move into a better position for delivery.

RELAXATION BASICS

You can use relaxation techniques all of the time, not just in labor. You'll find they help in many situations, from going to the dentist to coping with the demands of your new baby. There are a number of things you can do to make relaxing easier.

Get comfortable.

Wear comfortable, preferably loose, clothing. Sit or lie in a position where you won't feel pinched. Seek quiet places. Listen to soothing music.

Practice regularly.

Practice relaxation techniques at least three times a week. Do it at the same time, whether that's early morning or before you go to bed.

Tell your partner what helps you relax and what distracts you.

Pay attention to the parts of your body that react to stress.

Does your neck ache? Do your legs get stiff?

Think of yourself in a calm place, where you are feeling peaceful.

Imagining that you are relaxed may help you be relaxed. Some people find it helpful to imagine themselves in a particular place—lying on a warm beach, walking in a quiet forest, sitting on a mountaintop—that means "peace" to them.

Staying as relaxed as possible will help you feel more comfortable and may make your labor move along more quickly. Ways to stay relaxed include going for a walk, getting a massage, taking a warm bath or shower, "slow dancing" with your partner, or even humming or moaning a "labor song."

Many women feel that a rhythmic activity like swaying or rocking in a rocking chair is relaxing. Remember to breathe at a comfortable depth and rate.

Your partner can help you by encouraging you to relax and breathe properly and by caressing you while supporting your body.

LABOR AND CHILDBIRTH

THERE ARE three stages of labor, and three phases—early, active, and transition—during the first stage. (For specific information on each stage of labor, see the charts on pages 82 and 83.)

FIRST STAGE OF LABOR

What do "dilation" and "effacement" mean?

During the first stage of labor, the opening to your cervix is thinning out (effacing) and opening up (dilating) so that your baby can be born. The thinning, or **effacement**, is usually described in percentages. If your health care provider says you are 50 percent effaced, it means that the cervix has thinned to half its normal thickness. The opening, or **dilation**, is usually described in centimeters—10 centimeters would be fully dilated.

For some women, effacement and dilation may start days before they are ready to give birth, and proceed very slowly. For others, it may happen in a matter of hours.

Your health care provider may refer to **station**, or how low your baby is in your pelvis. When the baby's head is engaged at **zero station**, your baby is ready to move through the pelvic opening.

Effacement

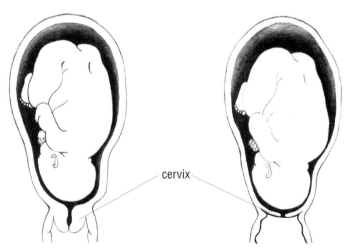

cervix

The mother's cervix "effaces," or thins, as the body prepares for birth. The illustration on the left shows a cervix that is not effaced yet, although the baby's head is pushing down. The cervix on the right is fully, or 100 percent, effaced.

When your labor begins, you may feel excited and relieved that it's finally time to have the baby. A warm bath (as long as your water hasn't broken), a cup of tea, a walk, slow dancing, or a massage may help you relax, and your partner can help you with these. Every woman is different, so pay attention to what makes you feel most comfortable.

Stations of Engagement

The baby's head is "engaged" when it is deep in the pelvic cavity. This illustration shows the "stations" of engagement. When the head is fully engaged, it is at zero station.

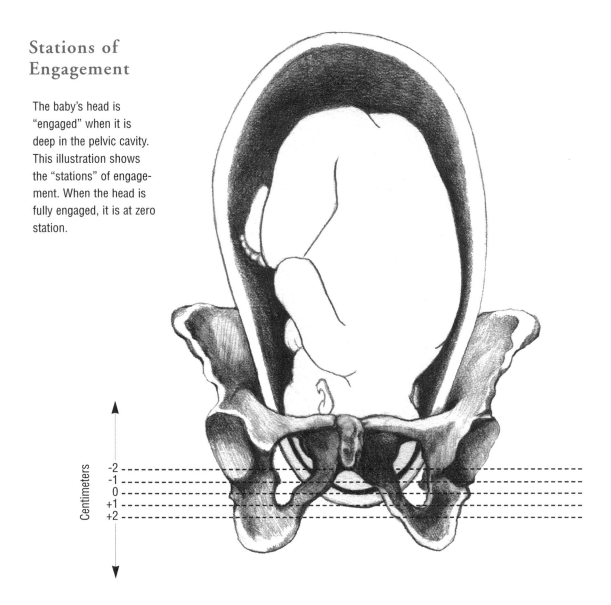

How dilated your cervix is when you arrive at the hospital depends on your pain tolerance, how far you have to travel, and how strong the contractions are. Usually your contractions are strong and frequent—it's normal to feel a little doubt about whether you can handle even stronger and more frequent contractions.

Use whatever breathing seems to work. Just remember to keep breathing and to use the relaxation techniques you learned in classes and have been practicing at home. While you may have felt lively and sociable during the early phase, now you will find yourself focusing on how you can get comfortable.

Transition Phase

What happens during the transition phase?

As your cervix dilates from 8 to 10 centimeters, your contractions will become quite strong, one right after another. You may be restless, perspiring, nauseated, hot, cold, or tense. Your body is working hard, and it takes a lot of effort to stay calm and to breathe through the contractions.

It may be hard for you to follow instructions right now. You are very focused on getting through each contraction.

This is the hardest part of labor for many women. You may worry that you can't keep going. It *will* be over soon. It may be helpful to remember that every contraction brings you closer to being done with labor and able to see your new baby.

Your birth partner and your health care providers will be supporting, encouraging, and calming you during this difficult stage. The more you have practiced your relaxation and breathing exercises, the better able you will be to cope right now.

As the transition phase ends, you may begin to feel like pushing or bearing down, rather than continuing your regular breathing. Tell your birth partner and health care provider that you have this feeling. Your birth partner can help you with breathing the short puffs that help prevent pushing before it is time.

Pain Management Options

You may feel so uncomfortable as your contractions increase that you need some kind of medication to help you with the pain. During the early phases of labor, your health care provider may encourage you to use relaxation and breathing rather than drugs, in order to minimize any effect the pain reliever may have on your baby before birth.

Medications you might receive during labor and delivery include **sedatives, systemic analgesic** (or pain relievers), **intrathecal analgesia, epidural analgesia,** or **general anesthesia.** All of these medications have benefits and drawbacks. The chart here gives you an idea of what these medications are.

TYPE	BENEFITS	DRAWBACKS
Sedative	Can relieve tension and help with rest and relaxation. Sometimes given early in labor to help a tired mother sleep. Helps relieve nausea and vomiting.	May cause dizziness, disorientation, dry mouth, or a drop in the mother's blood pressure.
Systemic Analgesic (Pain relievers)	Lessens pain and can help relaxation. Given during active labor.	May slow labor. If given too close to delivery, may cause slow breathing, poor sucking, or decreased muscle tone in newborn. This medication is unlikely to be used during transition or pushing.
Intrathecal Analgesia	A small amount of medication is injected into the spinal area by the anesthesiologist. Pain relief is often immediate and thorough. There is no numbing, so mother can be active after the injection. Pushing urges are felt.	May cause itching, nausea, or urinary retention in the mother. Medication can help control side effects.
Epidural Analgesia	Similar to intrathecal analgesia. A catheter is inserted into a space around the spine. Medication may be given all at once or continuously. Provides thorough pain relief.	I.V. fluids are given. The mother is numb from naval to mid-thigh and likely to stay in bed after injection. Decreased urge to push, which may result in use of forceps or vacuum extractor. Electronic fetal monitoring must be used.
Spinal Anesthesia	Used only for cesarean birth. Produces complete numbness from breastline to toes. Mother will be awake and comfortable for the birth.	May cause a drop in mother's blood pressure, nausea, or vomiting. Side effects for mother may be relieved with medication.
General Anesthesia	Used for fast cesarean delivery in case of emergency. Given by injection or inhalation. Mother quickly becomes unconscious.	Nausea or vomiting may occur. Mother not awake for birth. May cause respiratory distress, less vigorous suck, or poor muscle tone in baby for a short time after birth.

SECOND STAGE OF LABOR

In this stage, you begin to push and deliver your baby.

Once your cervix is fully opened, you may feel an overwhelming urge to push, as if your body is making all the decisions and the rest of you is just following along. This is hard work, but it can also be a relief: NOW you're going to have a baby.

Pushing often feels like having a very large bowel movement—and the pushing itself can sometimes cause you to have one. Don't worry about it; this is normal and may be a sign you are pushing well.

With help from your birth partner and health care providers, find a position that feels comfortable while you push. If you squat or stand, gravity will help the baby descend as you push, but for some women, squatting or standing is too hard on their legs. You may sit, in a regular chair or on a special birthing stool. If you want to lie down, try lying on your side with your upper leg supported by your birth partner, rather than on your back.

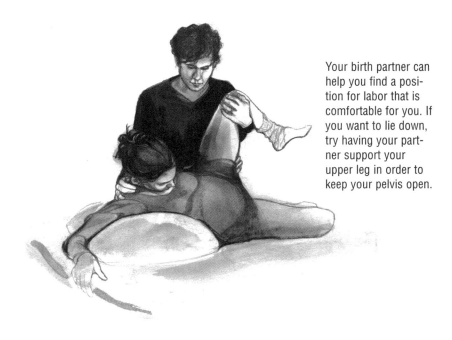

Your birth partner can help you find a position for labor that is comfortable for you. If you want to lie down, try having your partner support your upper leg in order to keep your pelvis open.

Once you have begun serious pushing, things may move fairly quickly. You are so focused on pushing and having this baby that you may barely hear what anyone says to you, and you will not pay much attention to anything else going on in the room.

Pushing time for a woman having her first baby is usually one to two hours. It's about a half hour less for women who have already had at least one baby.

In a normal birth, the baby will be born head first. The top of the head will begin to show as you push with contractions. **Crowning** is when the widest part of the baby's head is out of your body.

If an **episiotomy**—a surgical cut to enlarge the birth opening—is needed, it's done as the baby's head crowns. An episiotomy can help the baby be born faster, if there is some difficulty in the birth process. Many women can give birth without tearing or an episiotomy.

After the baby's head is delivered, the shoulders will emerge. Then the rest of the baby's body almost slips out.

Your health care provider will clamp and cut the umbilical cord that connects your baby to the placenta. (Often your birth partner will be offered the opportunity to do this.)

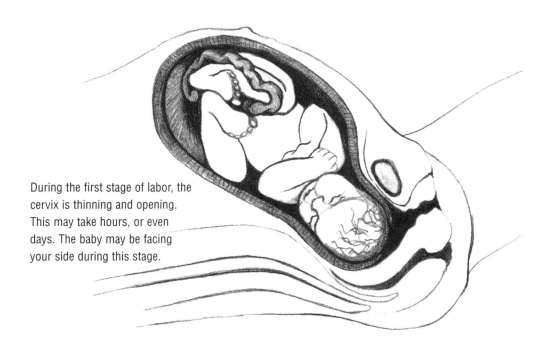

During the first stage of labor, the cervix is thinning and opening. This may take hours, or even days. The baby may be facing your side during this stage.

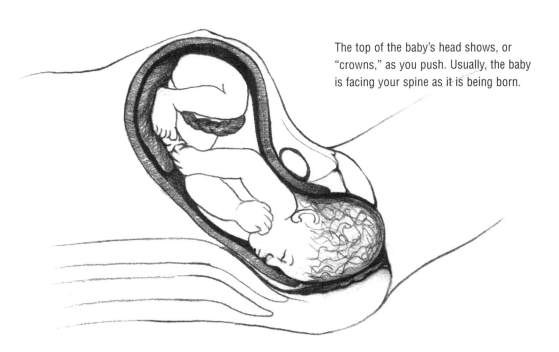

The top of the baby's head shows, or "crowns," as you push. Usually, the baby is facing your spine as it is being born.

In most births, the baby's head is delivered first, and takes the most effort.

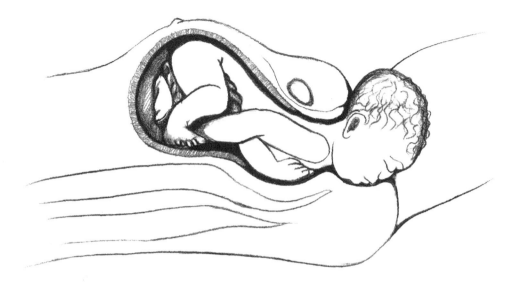

Once the head and shoulders are delivered, the rest of the baby's body come out easily.

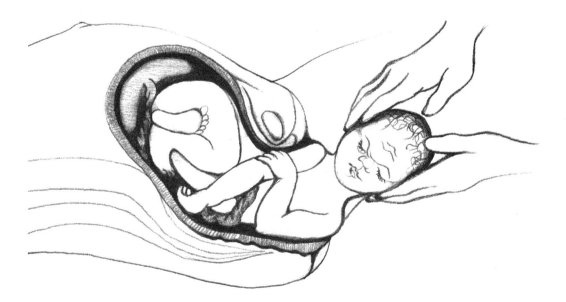

LABOR AND DELIVERY

FIRST STAGE: Dilation and Effacement of the Cervix (4-20 hours)

PHASES	LENGTH[1]	CONTRACTIONS	POSSIBLE EMOTIONAL, PHYSICAL SIGNS	PARTNER'S ROLE	COMFORT MEASURES
Early Dilation 0-4 cm Effacement 0-60%	1st baby 8-10 hours 2nd+ baby 4-6 hours	Intensity: mild Length: 30-45 seconds Interval: 5-20 minutes (irregular)	Abdominal cramps Intensity increases when activity increases Backache Bloody show Leak or rupture of BOW[2] Diarrhea Excitement Anxiety	Entertainment Help with relaxation Prepare for hospital trip Time contractions Keep calm Notify midwife/doctor Back pressure	Maintain normal activity as possible Bath or shower Comfortable position Pelvic rocking Back pressure Light diet Standing/walking
Active Dilation 4-8 cm Effacement 60-100%	1st baby 3-6 hours 2nd + baby 2-4 hours	Intensity: more painful, closer and longer Length: 50-60 seconds Interval: 2-5 minutes	Pain/pressure in hips, groin, back of legs Hot flashes/chills Increased bloody show Leak or rupture of BOW Thirsty Nausea, vomiting Harder to relax More quiet, "inward focus" Restless Feeling dependent	Stay close and calm Help with relaxation Time contractions Encourage position changes Wipe forehead with cool cloth Offer ice chips/fluids Constant encouragement After each exam, ask about progress Consider bath/shower Foot rubs, massages Help establish/protect rituals	Rituals Rhythmic movement Relaxation Empty bladder Change position Pelvic rocking Suckers/hard candy/popsicles Cool cloth Backrub Slow chest breathing Focal point Consider medication
Transition 8-10 cm	1st baby 1/2-3 hours 2nd+ baby 1/2-2 hours	Intensity: very strong Length: 70-90 seconds Interval: 1 1/2 to 2 min.	Very hard contractions Amnesia between contractions Leg cramps Backache Urge to push Nausea and vomiting Chills/hot flashes Shaking of legs Demanding, exhausted, vulnerable, scared, panicky	Offer encouragement Breathe with mom Backrub Supply dry pads Time contractions Simple clear directions Acknowledge her pain, have confidence that she can cope Notify staff if she wants to push	Take one contraction at a time Position changes/relaxation Backrub Cool cloth/fanning Ice chips/sips of water Socks/warm blanket Be open to support from caregiver and partners

[1] Lengths of time are averages. Your labor may be faster or slower and still be normal.
[2] BOW = "Bag of waters," or amniotic membrane.

SECOND STAGE: Delivery of Baby

LENGTH	CONTRACTIONS	POSSIBLE EMOTIONAL, PHYSICAL SIGNS	PARTNER'S ROLE	COMFORT MEASURES
1st baby 1/2-3 hours 2nd+ baby 1/2-1 hour	Intensity: may be mild at first, increased intensity over time Length: 60 seconds Interval: 3-5 minutes	Urge to push/rectal pressure Backache Stretching, burning, stinging sensation in perineum Confusion Fatigue	Help with position/body support Fan mom Cool cloth, ice chips Encourage relaxation between contractions Praise mom Prepare camera, etc. Ask to assist with delivery or cut cord, if you wish Enjoy birth	Listen to your body's urges Relax pelvic floor Adjust position for comfort, effective pushing Look at or touch baby's head Work with caregivers Pant to avoid pushing, or push as directed to do so Cool cloth, ice chips

THIRD STAGE: Delivery of Placenta

LENGTH	CONTRACTIONS	POSSIBLE EMOTIONAL, PHYSICAL SIGNS	PARTNER'S ROLE	COMFORT MEASURES
2-45 minutes	Intensity: usually mild (contractions may be stronger with 2nd+ baby) Length: irregular Interval: irregular	Relief May cry Desire to hold baby or simply rest	Praise mom Hold and enjoy baby Encourage mom to relax Look at placenta if desired Share in the joy and excitement	Push as directed to birth the placenta Breastfeeding Relax and rest Hold baby, if desired

FOURTH STAGE: Recovery

LENGTH	CONTRACTIONS	POSSIBLE EMOTIONAL, PHYSICAL SIGNS	PARTNER'S ROLE	COMFORT MEASURES
1-2 hours	Intensity: mild Length: short Interval: irregular	Relief, happiness Abdominal cramps (especially when breastfeeding) Lochia (blood discharge) Hunger, thirst Dizziness Curiosity about baby	Be proud of yourself and mom Telephone calls to family and friends Share feelings about the birth Help position baby for nursing Enjoy closeness with mom and baby Help screen visitors and calls	Breastfeeding Sponge bath Ice chips on bottom Food Position changes Rest and relaxation

THIRD STAGE OF LABOR

The **placenta**, often called the **afterbirth**, is expelled a few minutes after your baby is born. You will have a few contractions, usually painless. Your health care provider will watch for signs that the placenta is ready to be delivered, and may ask you to push a little to help expel it. As the placenta is expelled, you may feel a little pressure.

Immediately after Birth

Health care providers attending the birth will suction the baby's nose and mouth gently if needed and will make sure your baby is breathing well. The baby will be placed on your abdomen so you can see, touch, and bond with your new child. Often the baby is placed at your breast to begin nursing.

If you have had an episiotomy or a tear in your vagina, your health care provider will stitch you up after the delivery of the placenta. You will be given a local anesthetic similar to Novocaine so you will not feel the stitching.

Apgar Scale

A quick rating, called the **Apgar Scale**, is given right at birth, then again 5 minutes later, to measure how well the baby is doing after labor and delivery. The baby is given a "score" of 0 to 2 on 5 different aspects of its condition: heart rate, breathing, muscle tone, skin color, and reflex response.

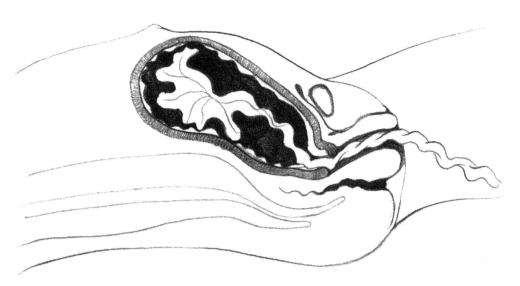

The placenta is delivered shortly after the baby is born.

CESAREAN BIRTH

A CESAREAN BIRTH—often referred to simply as a **C-section**—may be needed if the baby is in an abnormal position or if the mother or baby show signs of problems during labor. Your health care provider will help you decide whether a C-section is necessary. Once the decision to proceed with a C-section is made, you will be moved quickly to an operating area.

During a C-section, a doctor makes an incision in your abdomen and into the uterus and then removes the baby through the incision. In most cases, you will have regional anesthesia that numbs you but does not put you to sleep. If the doctor feels your baby needs to be delivered very quickly, you might be given general anesthesia, and you will not be awake as the baby is born.

After the birth, your uterus and then your abdomen will be stitched closed by the doctor.

Your birth partner will usually be able to be with you during the C-section, if the hospital and your health care provider allow it—and if your birth partner is comfortable with the idea.

Because of the skill of the doctors and nurses, and the use of modern medical equipment, most mothers and babies do well after the operation. Your recovery will be slower than it would be after a vaginal birth; you have just had abdominal surgery, and those tissues and muscles need time to heal again.

If you've been planning for a vaginal delivery, you may feel that a C-section is somehow a "failure." This just isn't true. A C-section can quickly relieve problems you or your baby may be having during the birth process. Except in rare emergencies, you and your birth partner will be fully involved in deciding whether to have a C-section. A C-section may offer the best opportunity for you and your baby to have a safe and healthy birth.

Having a C-section doesn't necessarily mean that your next baby will have to be delivered by C-section, too. You should discuss vaginal delivery for your next pregnancy with your health care provider.

What happens with a C-section?

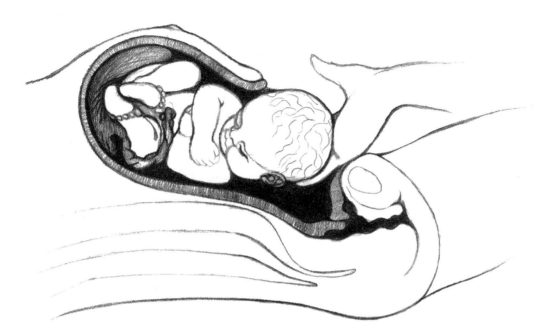

In a C-section, the baby is delivered through an incision in the abdomen and the uterus. Except in an emergency, the mother can be awake during the birth, and a partner may be present.

Your Hospital Stay

YOU MAY STAY in the hospital only a couple of days, but even a short stay should be as comfortable as possible.

Sleep and rest are very important after you've delivered your baby. You may feel excited and wide awake for a while, but remember that your body has been working hard and needs time to recover.

If you have visitors in the hospital, try to keep their visits short and don't feel that you have to entertain them.

Safety and Security

You, your baby, and your birth partner will have been "banded" right after birth, with matching identification bands attached to your wrist and your baby's wrist or ankle. The bands will be checked frequently while you are in the hospital.

Although incidents are extremely rare, for security reasons you should not hand your baby to anyone in the hospital who doesn't identify himself or herself and who isn't wearing an identification badge. If you have any hesitation or doubts, call for a nursing supervisor.

Your baby may stay in the room with you—keeping your baby with you as much as possible will help you learn more about the baby—but if you leave the room, even just to take a quick shower, do not leave the baby alone.

Hospital Routines

During your hospital stay you can expect that:

- **Several nurses will care for you, as work shifts change every 8 to 12 hours.** They will check on your recovery progress a few times each day. They also will help you with breastfeeding and give you information about caring for yourself and your baby at home.
- **Someone from the lab will draw blood from you and your baby.**
- **Your health care provider will visit you several times during your stay and talk to you about when you can go home.**
- **Your baby's health care provider will examine your baby several times, talk with you, and decide when your baby can go home.**
- **A representative from a photography firm may talk to you about ordering photos of your baby.** This is optional; you do not have to buy any photos.
- **If you have Rh-negative blood and received Rhogam at about 28 weeks of pregnancy, you may receive another injection before you leave the hospital.**
- **If you are not immune to Rubella (German measles), you will have a shot to protect any future babies.**

Postpartum Care

After your baby is born, your body begins its recovery. It doesn't recover all at once, but it does change noticeably right away. Just as you paid attention to the needs of your body during pregnancy, it's important to pay attention to those needs now.

Activity

Rest is very important. Your baby's needs will disrupt your sleep during a time when you could use a little more sleep than usual. Let other people—your partner, your mother, friends, relatives—help you.

You can do many of your daily activities at home, but do them one by one. Give yourself time for naps during the day when your baby is sleeping. Avoid lifting anything heavy or doing strenuous work or sports.

If you had a cesarean birth, you should not vacuum, drive a car, or climb a lot of stairs for 2 to 3 weeks.

Vaginal Flow, Menstruation

Right after a vaginal birth, your vaginal flow will be bright red. It should become dark red before you leave the hospital. If you see large clots (bigger than half dollars) or smell a bad odor, be sure to tell the nursing staff.

Your vaginal flow may continue for 4 to 6 weeks after giving birth. Usually the amount decreases and the color gets lighter. If you have been too active, your flow may become a brighter red and grow heavier for a while. If you need more than one pad an hour, lie down, rest, and call your clinic.

Menstrual periods usually start again 6 to 8 weeks after delivery. If you are breastfeeding, you may not have a menstrual period until you stop nursing. You can still get pregnant, however.

Perineal Care

Use the peri-bottle you got in the hospital and change sanitary pads every time you go to the bathroom. Take as many warm tub baths as you like to ease any pain. Do not use tampons or douches until vaginal bleeding has stopped.

Incision Care

After a cesarean birth, you can shower, but try to keep water off your incision. If the "steri-strip" tapes on your incision come loose, they can be taken off after you've been home for a week. Gently pull both ends of the strip toward the incision. You may see a small amount of clear or pink drainage. Check with your health care provider if the drainage increases or has an odor, if the incision reddens, or if you have a fever.

Bowels/Hemorrhoids

Reduce your risk of constipation, which is common after childbirth, by drinking plenty of fluids—6 to 8 glasses of non-caffeinated liquids every day—and by increasing the amount of fiber in your diet. If hemorrhoids are a problem, warm tub baths are soothing. Try not to strain when you have a bowel movement. Your health care provider can recommend an over-the-counter medication to help with constipation.

NUTRITION

Keep up the good eating habits you developed during pregnancy. Eat a well-balanced diet that includes foods from every part of the food pyramid (see pages 8-9). Don't try to lose your pregnancy weight quickly by cutting back on calories.

KEGELS

Those Kegel exercises you were doing during pregnancy are still useful. (In fact, they are useful throughout your life.) After having a baby, you may barely be able to feel the muscles, but if you keep doing the Kegels, you are less likely to leak urine when you sneeze or cough.

SEX

Sexual intercourse should be avoided for at least 3 to 4 weeks after delivery, or until the brownish-red vaginal flow is completely gone. Most health care providers recommend that you not have vaginal intercourse until after your post-delivery clinic visit. If you do, however, and you do not want to become pregnant again, you should use birth control. It's possible to get pregnant within a month after having a baby, even if you're breastfeeding.

WHEN TO CALL YOUR HEALTH CARE PROVIDER

- **If you have a temperature of 100.4° F or higher.**
- **If you have heavy vaginal bleeding, bright red bleeding saturating more than one pad an hour, or clots larger than a half dollar.**
- **If you have bleeding for more than 6 weeks.**
- **If you have burning or pain while urinating, or a frequent or urgent need to urinate.**
- **If you have pain in one spot or a red area on your breast.**
- **If you have foul-smelling vaginal discharge.**
- **If you have increased drainage, swelling, pain, or redness around your incision from a cesarean birth.**
- **If you have redness or pain around a vein in your leg, or if you can't stand on that leg.**
- **If you have extreme abdominal pain.**

EXERCISE

YES, YOU CAN start exercising soon after birth, but most health care providers recommend waiting about 6 weeks before starting any serious workouts. Begin exercising slowly, but make exercise a part of your daily routine. Remember, it took you months to gain your pregnancy weight and shape, and it will take months to lose them.

Start walking, a little bit at a time. This will help you feel better in general, although it won't work on specific muscles like the exercises described below or the ones illustrated on the opposite page.

ABDOMINAL TIGHTENING

What kind of exercise can I do after having a baby?

Lying on your back or side or, later, sitting or standing, take a deep breath in through your nose and feel your abdomen expand. Blow the air out slowly through your mouth while pulling your abdominal muscles in. Do this 2 to 3 times to start. You can do this exercise 24 hours after birth.

PELVIC TILT

Lie on your back with your knees bent. Flatten your lower back against the floor. While letting your breath out, tighten your abdominal muscles and then hold for 3 to 4 breaths. Relax and repeat.

Abdominal Crunches

Lie on your back with your knees bent. Put your arms in front of you, behind your neck, folded over your chest, at your side, or over your head. Tuck your chin to your chest, then roll your head and shoulders forward as far as you can without moving your waist off the floor. Roll back, relax, then repeat. Slowly increase the number of times you do this.

"Tippy Toes"

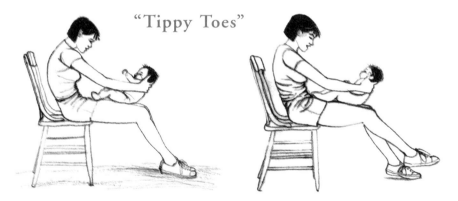

Sit on the edge of a straight-back chair with your legs forward and knees slightly bent. Hold the baby in your lap facing you. Round your upper back and contract your abdominal muscles. Slowly walk your feet out in front of you until only your toes touch the floor. Keeping your abdominal muscles contracted, lift one foot at a time about 2 to 3 inches off the floor. Repeat, alternating feet. This exercise helps strengthen abdominal muscles and relieve upper-back tension.

YOUR EMOTIONS

ALMOST ANYTHING you feel after your baby is born is normal—that is, other women often feel the same way.

What if I don't love
my baby right away?

You may feel an instant connection to your baby, but don't worry if you don't. For many women, the love and connection grows as they take care of their new baby for days or even weeks.

In the first 24 hours after birth, you will start learning how to take care of yourself and your baby: how to change diapers, how to give your baby a bath, and how to feed your baby. You may still be thinking about your labor and delivery. It can be hard to believe that your pregnancy is over and you actually have a baby now.

After a day or so, you will feel the bond between you and your baby strengthening. You begin to see your baby as a separate person, with a special personality and needs.

BABY BLUES

Many women find themselves feeling some amount of sadness and anxiety from 3 to 10 days after delivery. They may feel tired, irritable, sad, or confused. They may even feel guilty—"I have a wonderful baby, why do I feel so sad?"

Why do I feel sad?

It's normal to feel blue. Yout hormones are rapidly returning to pre-pregnancy levels, you are tired, and you aren't getting enough sleep. Having a baby, especially a first baby, changes your life. If you were working before the birth, now you may feel lonely being at home with just your baby for company most of the time.

The important thing is to talk to others: your partner, relatives, friends, your health care provider. Ask for help so you can get more rest and feel more confident about taking care of your baby.

POSTPARTUM DEPRESSION

If you feel blue for more than a few days—or if at any time you feel as if you are out of control and may harm yourself or your baby—get help right away. Call your health care provider. Postpartum depression is real and can be serious.

ADOPTION

If you placed your baby for adoption, you may feel a strong sense of grief after the birth. You may have sad feelings on holidays, birthdays, or even during a diaper commercial. Give yourself a chance to rest and heal. Ask your health care provider, social worker, or adoption agency for support groups or agencies that can help you express and accept your feelings of sadness, while supporting you in your decision.

CLINIC VISITS

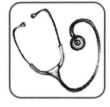

YOU WILL BE asked to see your health care provider 2 to 6 weeks after giving birth. At this visit, you may have some blood drawn and your urine tested, and you'll have a physical, including a pelvic exam. If you have not had a Pap smear for a year or more, your health care provider will take one.

At the exam, your health care provider will discuss family planning options with you and will answer any questions you have about exercise and other physical activities.

As noted earlier, most health care providers recommend that you not have vaginal intercourse until after your post-delivery clinic visit. If you do, however, and you do not want to become pregnant again, you should use birth control. It's possible to get pregnant within a month after having a baby, even if you're breastfeeding.

FOR PARTNERS

YOUR HELP is essential throughout the birth process—and maybe even more important afterwards. The birth of a baby is an exciting and wonderful time for both you and your partner. There is nothing quite like the experience of welcoming a new little person into the world.

If you've gone through childbirth classes with your partner, you already know what you can do during labor and birth: helping with breathing, saying encouraging words, giving massages, supporting her as she gets into position to deliver the baby.

Maybe this makes you a little nervous. After all, you've probably never been present for a birth before. What if you faint? What if you can't handle it? It's normal to be nervous. If you have very strong fears, talk with your partner long before the baby's due date so you have a back-up plan, such as another relative or friend to be a birth partner if needed.

You and your partner may want to consider hiring a professional support person, called a **doula**, to help with labor. A doula is specially trained to assist women and their partners before, during, and after birth. The doula is not there to take your place but rather to help you and your partner during this important event. Ask your health care provider for a list of doulas in your area.

Your partner will need a lot of support after giving birth. She's still recovering physically, and she also needs emotional support. She may get the "baby blues," and she can use some reassurance from you. After the birth you can help by burping the baby, changing diapers, giving the baby a bath, and so on. You and your partner can share caring for the baby, delighting in every little thing he or she does.

FOR MORE INFORMATION

See the list of resources at the end of the previous chapter.

Your Newborn

This tiny creature in your arms is your baby—no longer a bulge in your belly, but an independent little person who cries and squirms and eats and sleeps. You're excited and scared—this baby is so small—and amazed at just how much there is to know about your newborn.

SOME OF THE QUESTIONS ANSWERED IN THIS CHAPTER INCLUDE:

- What about those funny spots?
- What can my baby see and hear?
- What's the best way to keep my baby clean?
- How do I change a diaper?
- Is all this crying normal?
- How do I make sure the baby's crib is safe?
- When do I call my health care provider?

A First Look at Your Newborn

YOU MAY THINK your newborn is the most beautiful baby—the most beautiful anything—you've ever seen.

Then again, you might not. Your baby's head may have been squeezed into a long shape during the birth process. Or, if forceps were used, there may be red marks on the sides of your baby's head. Maybe your baby has long, fine hair over his or her body.

These characteristics are all completely normal—and temporary. The forceps marks will fade away and the baby's head will round into a normal shape in a few days. The long, fine hair, called **lanugo**, will disappear in about a week.

Other things you may notice about your newborn:

Head

- There are soft spots on the top and at the back of your baby's head, where the bones still haven't grown together. These soft spots may make you a little nervous about touching your baby's head. You need to be gentle, but you can still wash your baby's hair or massage your baby's head and scalp.
- There may be a soft, spongy area on your baby's head, caused by the pressure of birth. This will go away in a few days. Some babies have a hard knot on the top of their head, called a **cephalhematoma**. This will also go away, although it may take 4 to 6 months.

Eyes

- Light-skinned babies usually have grayish-blue eyes when they are born. Dark-skinned babies usually have grayish-brown eyes. Your baby's true eye color may appear in a few months, or may take as long as a year to develop. The color of your baby's eyes doesn't have anything to do with the ability to see.

NOSE

- Some babies are born with a nose that looks squished. The nose will develop normally in a short time.
- Your baby may sneeze a lot. The inside of the nose is much smaller than the nostrils you see, so mucus catches easily. Sneezing clears the nasal passages so the baby can breathe.

SKIN

- Small white bumps called **milia** are common on the face. Just leave them alone—don't try to squeeze or pick at them—and they will disappear in a few weeks.
- Some babies will have a newborn rash on their bodies. It will disappear in about a week.
- **Stork bites** are flat, red areas around the baby's head, neck, or eyelids. Sometimes they get redder when the baby cries. They should disappear within a year.
- Dark-skinned babies may have a darker area on their buttocks, back, or genitals that can be present for 4 or 5 years. This **Mongolian Spot** is not harmful and doesn't hurt, even though it may look like a bruise.

GENITALS

- Both boy and girl babies usually have swollen genitals. This is sometimes startling to parents, but it's normal and the swelling goes down in a few days.

What about those funny spots?

Some of the unusual marks you notice on your newborn baby's body, such as a squished nose or red "stork bite" are normal and will change or disappear as your baby matures.

WHAT YOUR NEWBORN CAN DO

ALTHOUGH YOUR baby needs your protection and care, he or she was born with the ability to do a number of things. You'll enjoy watching and playing with your baby, and your attention will help your baby develop.

WHAT YOUR BABY CAN SEE

- When first born, a baby can see about a foot away. By the time the baby is 4 to 6 months old, he or she can see as well as an adult. Babies like faces, so looking into your baby's eyes and talking will often fascinate your baby.
- Babies can get overwhelmed by having too much to look at. Keep your baby's sleeping area uncluttered. Very bright colors in decorating or bedding can be too exciting for a new baby.

WHAT YOUR BABY CAN HEAR

- Your baby was able to hear even before birth, and has probably learned your voice while in the uterus. When your baby is born, he or she can hear as well as an adult.
- Your baby will get used to the normal sounds of your household. You shouldn't play your stereo at the loudest volume, but no one needs to tiptoe or whisper.
- The high-pitched "baby talk" voice we often use with babies is something they seem to like. A baby will turn toward someone using that voice and study the speaker's face.

WHAT YOUR BABY CAN SMELL AND TASTE

- Newborn babies can smell as well as an adult, and their sense of taste is even stronger than that of adults.
- A baby will turn away from sharp, unpleasant odors.
- Babies like sweet things—like the taste of a mother's breast milk. You should never add sugar to a baby's formula or water, however, because it can cause diarrhea.

WHAT YOUR BABY CAN FEEL

- Babies need to be held, to feel close to someone, and to be touched by loving hands. Fussiness with diaper changes or baths is normal; don't let it keep you from holding your baby.
- You can keep your newborn with you most of the time.

What can my baby see and hear?

Don't worry about "spoiling" your baby by holding or carrying him or her too much. The warmth of your body, and your particular scent, are very soothing.

REFLEXES

- You may have seen your baby's **sucking reflex** just after he or she was born. When put to your breast, your baby opened his or her mouth, attached to your nipple, and began to suck.

- The **rooting reflex** works with the sucking reflex to make sure a newborn gets fed. You can see your baby's rooting reflex by stroking his or her cheek. The baby's head will turn toward the side you touched.

- Touch the bottom of your newborn's feet, and the toes will curl in. Put a finger in your baby's hand, and the fingers will curl in as well. This **grasp reflex** disappears over about 4 months. By that time, your baby will be able to grab your finger—and anything else he or she wants—by choice.

What reflexes does my baby have?

- In the first few weeks, your baby may often exhibit a **startle reflex** when moved suddenly. When your baby "startles," he or she will throw open the arms and hands, then bring them back in. This reflex disappears in about 3 months.

- Many proud parents try to show off their newborn's "walking." This is just an early reflex, not a sign that your baby is ready to walk. If you hold your baby up, feet touching a surface, the baby will take "steps" on the surface.

- If your baby is lying stomach down and you put your hand against the bottoms of his or her feet, you'll see your baby push forward against your hand. This early **crawling reflex** can move a tiny infant quickly across a flat surface. Never leave your baby alone on a high, flat surface.

CIRCUMCISION

YOU MAY WISH to have your baby boy's penis circumcised. In this procedure, the foreskin—the skin that covers the head of the penis—is cut away. Some parents choose circumcision for religious reasons, others because they think it is the "usual" thing to do.

Although physicians once routinely recommended circumcision for health reasons, many physicians now see it as an elective procedure—one that parents may choose, but that is not necessary for the baby's health. If you are considering circumcision, ask your health care provider to talk with you about the risks and the current medical thinking.

If you choose to have your baby circumcised, the procedure usually will be done before you leave the hospital. The surgery takes about 10 minutes, and healing generally takes about a week.

KEEPING YOUR BABY CLEAN

YOUR NEWBORN only needs to be bathed once or twice a week, but you need to clean his or her bottom throughout the day and comb the scalp once a day.

CORD CARE

- You should clean the cord once a day. The cord should fall off 1 to 3 weeks after birth. Continue to clean the area where the cord was attached until it heals. To clean the cord and the cord area, first wash your hands, then dip a cotton swab in alcohol and very gently rub around the base of the cord. Pull the cord up and push the cotton swab gently into the base to remove any secretions.
- To keep the cord dry, fold the diaper below the cord during the first few weeks.
- If the cord area looks red, you notice a bad smell, or you see pus in the cord area, call your health care provider. These are signs of an infection.

NAIL CARE

- Babies' fingernails can be sharp. They are very soft and hard to cut for at least 2 to 3 weeks. You can gently file them.

GENITAL CARE

- Girls sometimes have a small pink or white discharge from the vagina. This is normal and nothing to worry about. Always wash a girl's genital area from front to back.
- If your baby boy is circumcised, check every day to make sure you can see the rim of the mushroom-like head of the penis. If you can't, call the baby's health care provider during office hours. For the first 2 or 3 days only, protect the circumcised penis from sticking to the diaper by putting a small dab of petroleum jelly on the tip of the penis with each diaper change. (Using petroleum jelly longer than 2 or 3 days may inhibit the healing process.) Clean the circumcised penis with plain water. If you notice bleeding or pus, or if your baby seems to be having trouble passing urine, contact your health care provider immediately.

What's the best way to keep my baby clean?

• If your baby is not circumcised, clean the penis gently with water, but do not pull on the foreskin.

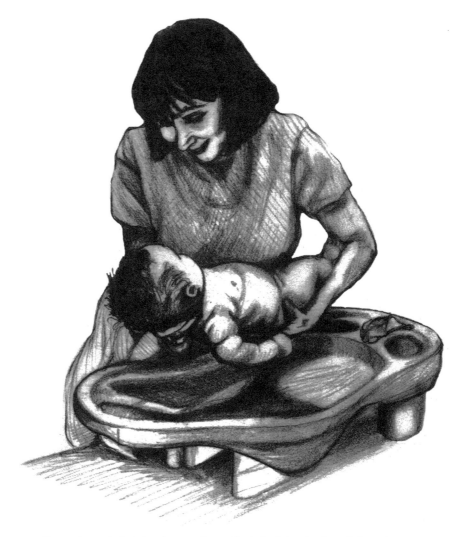

Support your baby's head as you lower the baby into a basin or tub, and as you gently bathe each part of your baby's body.

GIVING YOUR BABY A BATH

DON'T PUT your baby into a sink or pan of water until after the cord falls off. Until then, you can bathe your baby with a warm, wet washcloth while he or she is lying on a safe surface.

Whether your baby is being bathed in water or while lying on a safe surface, you should make sure he or she doesn't get chilled. Keep the area warm, and wrap your baby in warm, dry clothes right after the bath.

1. Gather bath supplies together. These include:
   • mild soap (although you can bathe your baby in warm water without soap)
   • alcohol and cotton swabs
   • comb and brush
   • clean diaper
   • clean clothes
   • washcloth and towels
   • pan or sink for water
   • a safe surface, with a blanket or pad

2. Test the water for the bath. It should be warm, but not hot. Use your elbow to check for a safe water temperature. Never put your baby into a bath without checking the water first.

3. When your baby's cord has fallen off, you can put him or her into the water. While supporting your baby's head with your hand, lower your baby's body into the water.

4. Wash around the eyes first with plain water. Then wash the face with plain water. Don't use cotton swabs to clean your baby's nose or ears.

5. Wash the baby's hair with plain water or with water and a mild shampoo. After the bath, comb your baby's scalp to remove oily build-up.

6. Wash your baby's stomach, back, and hands with plain water. If the cord is still on, clean it with alcohol and a cotton swab. Clean between your baby's fingers.

7. Wash the legs and feet, including between the toes.

8. Wash the baby's bottom from front to back with water and mild soap.

TAKING YOUR BABY'S TEMPERATURE

ALTHOUGH A **rectal temperature** is more accurate, it is safer and easier to take an **axillary temperature** for a newborn.

The axillary temperature is taken by tucking the thermometer into your baby's bare armpit and holding the arm gently against the chest. Hold the thermometer this way for at least 4 minutes. An average axillary temperature is 97.6° F.

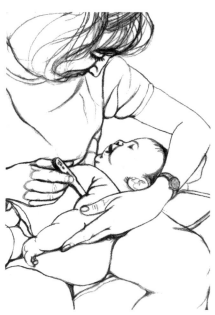

Take an axillary temperature by tucking the thermometer into your baby's bare armpit.

For a rectal temperature, lubricate the tip of a rectal thermometer (specially made, with a small, round bulb at the end) with petroleum jelly. Put your baby on his or her stomach, with a diaper underneath. (Taking a rectal temperature is likely to cause a bowel movement.) Or put the baby on his or her back and lift the baby's legs with one hand while pushing apart the buttocks with the other enough to see the rectum. Insert the thermometer gently, about a half inch. Hold it in place for about 3 minutes. An average rectal temperature is 99.6° F.

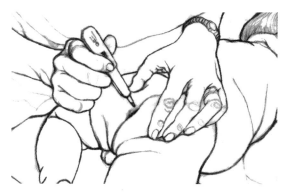

Take a rectal temperature by putting just the tip of a rectal thermometer into the baby's rectum.

USING THE BULB SYRINGE

YOU CAN USE a bulb syringe to clear your baby's nose and mouth of mucus, especially when your baby spits up, has a stuffy nose, or sneezes.

Squeeze the bulb of the syringe until it is collapsed. Gently place it just inside one of the baby's nostrils and quickly release the bulb. Then remove and clean the syringe by squeezing its contents into a tissue. Repeat for the other nostril, and for the mouth, if needed. Wash the syringe with soapy water and rinse after each use.

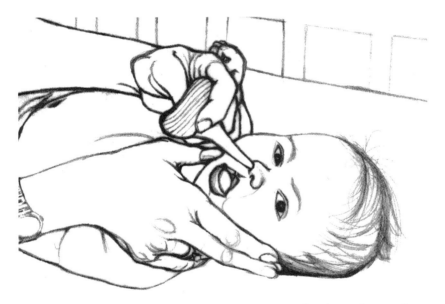

A bulb syringe is useful to clear your baby's nose and mouth at home. Squeeze the bulb and gently put it just inside your baby's nose, then release the bulb and remove it from your baby's nose.

DIAPERING

YOUR BIGGEST CONCERN about diapering may be whether to use cloth or disposable diapers. Disposable diapers are more expensive than cloth diapers you wash yourself. Cleaning cloth diapers may be more work than you want. If you are concerned about the environment, you may want to avoid disposables. But if you are going back to work soon and will leave your child in daycare, you may need to use disposables.

Whichever kind of diapers you choose, your baby may develop diaper rash from time to time. You can help prevent this by washing your baby's bottom with plain water each time you change a diaper, and by changing diapers often—every 3 hours or so.

How do I change a diaper?

BABY'S CRYING

NEWBORN BABIES tell you what they want by crying. They cry when they're hungry, tired, or uncomfortable. They cry when they've had too much excitement or not enough.

You can expect your baby to cry about 2 or 3 hours out of every day. Some days it may be more, and some days it may be less. Some things to remember:

- **Your baby cries because that's how he or she communicates.**
- **Responding to your baby's cries now may mean less crying in the future.**
- **A newborn baby can't be "spoiled" if you pick him or her up.** In some cultures, babies are held almost constantly by their mothers.
- **Your baby is different than anyone else's baby.** While some ways of dealing with crying may have worked for your sister's baby or your next-door-neighbor's baby, you have to learn what your baby needs.
- **Never handle your baby when you're feeling angry or frustrated.** Put the baby in a safe place, or let someone else hold the baby for a while, and then walk away and calm down.
- **Never shake your baby.**

Is all this crying normal?

THINGS YOU CAN TRY TO EASE YOUR BABY'S CRYING

- **Feed your baby.** Yes, even if it's only been a short time since the last feeding. Your baby has his or her own schedule that doesn't always follow a clock.
- **Rub the baby's tummy, or lay the baby over your arm or lap and rub his or her back.**
- **Get out the rocking chair.** Rock the baby, or walk around the room while holding the baby.
- **Check the baby's clothing.** Add a layer if it's chilly; take a layer off if it's hot.
- **Take a ride in the car, with the baby safely buckled into the infant car seat in the back.**
- **Let your baby cry for a few minutes.** Often babies cry to "blow off steam." This is normal and when it happens, nothing you do will stop the crying. It's fine to let your baby cry for 10 to 15 minutes, then try to soothe him or her. Then let him or her cry another 10 to 15 minutes, and try soothing again. Keep this up until the baby becomes sleepy or hungry and calms down.

Newborn Safety

You can help keep your baby safe by following these guidelines:

- **Always use a federally-approved car seat**—even when you give your baby his or her first ride home from the hospital. The safest place for the car seat is in the middle of the backseat, facing the rear of the car. Yes, that can be awkward, but it is one of the most important things you can do for your baby. *Never* hold your baby on your lap in a moving car.

- **Never leave your baby alone in a vehicle.** Not even "just for a minute" as you run into the house or a store to pick something up.

- **Never leave your baby alone on a high, flat surface, like the top of a dresser or changing table.** Even a very tiny baby can scoot across a flat surface if its feet find something to push against.

- **Put your baby to sleep on his or her back, not on the tummy.** Recent research has shown that babies who sleep on their sides or backs are less likely to have Sudden Infant Death Syndrome (SIDS).

- **Make sure your baby's crib is safe.** It should have slats that are no more than 2³⁄8 inches apart, and the mattress should fit snugly against the edge of the crib—you should not be able to to fit 2 fingers between the mattress and the side of the crib. If the crib is painted, make sure that lead-free paint was used. If you don't know, it's better to get a newer crib. Don't use bumper pads or pillows in the crib; babies can be suffocated in their soft surfaces. No toys should be left in the crib with a newborn. Keep the crib away from windows, plants, drapes, electric cords, or anything that the baby might be able to grasp.

- **Only use store-bought pacifiers.** This is one item that you should not try to make at home. Check the pacifier often by pulling on the bulb to make sure it's not loose, sticky, or cracked. If it is, replace it immediately.

How do I make sure
the baby's crib is safe?

- **Never prop a bottle for the baby to eat.** Always hold your baby while feeding.
- **Never microwave formula or breast milk.** It heats unevenly and may burn the inside of your baby's mouth.
- **Keep your baby out of direct sunlight—a newborn's skin is very sensitive—and don't use insect repellent or sunscreen on your baby for at least six months.**
- **Don't drink hot beverages, eat hot food, or smoke while holding your baby.**
- **Don't smoke around your baby.** Secondhand smoke can cause illnesses, including ear infections and breathing problems.

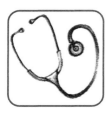

When do I call my
health care provider?

CLINIC VISITS

IF YOU HAVEN'T picked a health care provider for your baby
before birth, you should pick one as soon as your baby is born.

A visit to the health care provider usually is scheduled for 2
weeks after the baby is born. At this visit, the health care
provider will give you a schedule for regular check-ups for your
baby, including the immunizations he or she will need.

WHEN TO CALL YOUR HEALTH CARE PROVIDER

You may not be sure when your baby is sick and needs to see
a health care provider, especially if this is your first baby. Some
signs that your baby should see someone are:

- **An underarm (axillary) temperature higher than 100.5° F,
  or a rectal temperature higher than 101° F.**
- **Changes in your baby's behavior.** For example, a normally
  quiet baby is very fussy and irritable all day, or an active
  baby is very sleepy and limp.
- **Vomiting.** This is not spitting up after feedings, which is
  normal, but actually vomiting stomach contents.
- **Diarrhea or constipation.**
- **If your baby's skin seems yellow and your baby is very
  sleepy.**
- **If your baby's skin seems bluish, or if your baby starts
  coughing.**
- **If your baby is uninterested in feeding for more than 6 to 8
  hours.**

Don't hesitate to call your health care provider if you are
concerned about your baby's health. No one will think you're
foolish if you ask for help.

Neonatal Intensive Care Unit (NICU)

IF YOUR BABY needs special care, he or she will be taken care of in the intensive care nursery or special care unit, where the extra care gives your baby a better chance at a healthy future.

When you first look at the neonatal intensive care unit (NICU), you may think the machines and lights and sounds are frightening. The high-tech equipment doesn't look like what you thought would be your baby's first environment, but it's all there to meet your baby's special needs and to monitor his or her condition.

While your baby is in the NICU, the staff will provide you with information so you will understand what is happening to your baby and how well your baby is doing.

FOR PARTNERS

EXCEPT FOR breastfeeding, you can do everything your partner does now. You can hold, bathe, and diaper the baby. You can talk to him or her, hold the baby in your arms, or carry the baby in a front pack against your chest. You can make sure the baby is buckled into a babyseat when you're in the car, and you can check the baby's crib to make sure it's safe. And, if the baby is taking formula, you can even help feed the baby.

Get to know the baby, and the basics of baby care, so you can be actively involved in taking care of the baby. This will give your partner some relief, and it will be good for the baby. But you'll also find that it is good for you, too.

FOR MORE INFORMATION

The Amazing Newborn by Klaus and Klaus.

The Baby Book by William and Martha Sears.

Caring for Your Baby and Young Child by S. Shelov, MD, and R. Hesherman, MD

The Newborn Mother: Stages of Her Growth by Andrea Boroff Eagan.

On Becoming A Family by T. Berry Brazelton.

Touchpoints by T. Berry Brazelton.

What Every Baby Knows by T. Berry Brazelton.

You and Your Newborn Baby by Linda Todd.

7 *Feeding Your Baby*

Breastfeeding is, for most women, the best way to feed your baby. The milk your body provides is the best source of nutrition for your baby, and nursing can make you feel closer to your baby, while your baby feels protected and safe.

Although most women are able to breastfeed their babies, some cannot, for physical and other reasons. With today's prepared formula, you can still provide your baby with healthy food and a safe, warm experience while feeding.

**SOME OF THE QUESTIONS ANSWERED
IN THIS CHAPTER INCLUDE:**

- What are the advantages of breastfeeding?
- How often should I nurse my baby?
- Can I give my breastfed baby a bottle sometimes?
- Why do I have sore nipples?
- What if I want to bottlefeed my baby?
- What if my baby won't take the breast?
- How long can I keep formula?

BREASTFEEDING

BREASTFEEDING is a natural way to feed your baby. Most women can breastfeed, if they give it a try. After all, that's what your body was made to do. Breastfeeding is convenient: Your baby's food is always right there, there's nothing to prepare, and you have no bottles to wash.

Many women say that the closeness they feel while nursing a baby is something they could not have imagined. The connection is very powerful, and pleasurable. Nursing can force you to sit down for a while and just enjoy your baby and the pleasure of being a mother. It's easy to get caught up in all the things you need to do—taking care of your baby and your home and perhaps a job or other children. You end up doing chores, taking care of everything, while the days just slip by. You can't rush through breastfeeding, and that may help you find a peaceful moment for yourself as well as for your baby.

You can nurse your baby even if you plan to return to work. Breastfeeding for just a few weeks is healthier than not breastfeeding at all. But many women continue to nurse even after going back to work. Today's breast pumps make it easy to save milk for your baby, whether you can be there for every feeding or not.

Although breastfeeding is natural, it is a skill that you and your baby must practice. Before your baby is born, try to attend a breastfeeding class with your partner. Classes are usually offered by hospitals or by the La Leche League in your area.

THE BREAST

Your breasts changed a lot while you were pregnant. They got bigger and more tender. These changes were caused by the growth of the milk-producing cells and an increase in blood flow to the breasts. If you have lighter skin, you may even be able to see blue veins in your breasts now. Your nipples may have gotten much bigger and darker, and some funny bumps may have appeared in the areola part of the nipple. These bumps are actually small glands that help keep your nipples soft and protected from bacteria when you are nursing. Soap can destroy this protective effect, so wash your breasts only with warm water.

What are the advantages of breastfeeding?

Some women have a slight leaking of fluid from their breasts in the last months of pregnancy. This thick yellowish fluid, colostrum, is the first food your baby will have. Your breasts are producing it, even if you don't see it before your baby is born.

After your baby is born, your breasts will produce colostrum for 2 or 3 days. Colostrum gives your newborn protection against many diseases and helps the baby's body rid itself of **meconium**, the first black, tarry stools.

The delivery of the placenta, or afterbirth, stimulates your breasts to begin producing milk. Milk is produced in special cells of the breast, then released through the nipple. A special hormone causes the milk to be released. This effect is called the **let-down reflex.**

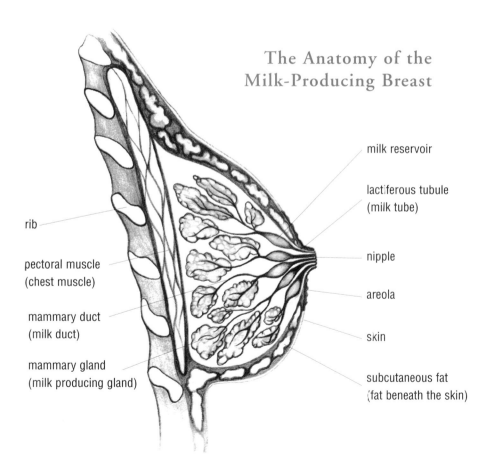

The Anatomy of the Milk-Producing Breast

milk reservoir

lactiferous tubule (milk tube)

rib

nipple

pectoral muscle (chest muscle)

areola

mammary duct (milk duct)

skin

mammary gland (milk producing gland)

subcutaneous fat (fat beneath the skin)

PREPARING FOR BREASTFEEDING

Your baby is ready to nurse at birth, but he or she may need a little help getting started. Getting your baby onto the breast is sometimes awkward at first. The nurses will be there to help you with this when your baby is first born.

For successful nursing, the first steps are:

- **Have a calm, pleasant place to nurse.** Create an area that you can think of as a nursing corner. Make sure you have a chair that is comfortable for you with a baby in your arms, in a relatively quiet part of your house. Your chair or sofa should be padded enough so you can get in a comfortable position and sit for a while.

To begin breastfeeding, find a comfortable position for you and your baby, with your back and arms supported. Bending your leg into a chair, or using a footstool, can help.

- **Massage your breasts.** Use the palm of your hand and gently push into your breast from underneath and move up towards the nipple. Then do the same from the sides and top.

- **Present your breast to the baby.** Hold your breast, usually with your thumb on top and fingers underneath, about an inch from the nipple. The palm of your hand will rest on your stomach, below the nipple. Your fingers will look something like a letter "C."
- **Get your baby to open his or her mouth.** Gently rub your nipple across the baby's lips. If you open your mouth wide and tell your baby to say "ah," he or she will seem to mimic you.
- **Make sure your baby is close enough.** When your baby's mouth opens, pull the baby close, so that your nipple and areola are deep in your baby's mouth. Don't lean towards the baby, pull the baby closer to your breast. Be sure your baby's nose, chest, and knees are touching you.

 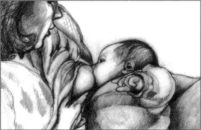

Use your free hand to partially circle the breast and guide it into your baby's mouth. Make sure you get all of the nipple and areole into the baby's mouth.

- **Do special massage with inverted nipples.** Many women have nipples that do not stick out far enough for a baby to nurse well. This problem can be corrected by various exercises, including the **Hoffman Technique.** To do this exercise, put the forefingers of each hand on opposite sides of your nipple, then pull back and stretch the skin. Now move your fingers to another position on the nipple and do it again, working your way around the whole nipple. Ask your health care provider or a **lactation consultant** (someone professionally trained to help women and babies with breastfeeding) for advice on how to deal with inverted nipples.

BREASTFEEDING POSITIONS

There are a number of positions for breastfeeding. Try several and see which are most comfortable for you and your baby.

Cradle Hold

This is the classic position for breastfeeding, but it may be awkward when you first start nursing your baby. In this position, you cradle your baby's head in the crook of the arm on the same side as the breast. If your baby is nursing from the left breast, his or her head will be resting in the crook of your left arm. Use your other hand to lift your breast, partly circling the nipple with the thumb on top and fingers underneath. Touch your baby's lip or the side of the mouth with the nipple so that he or she will open the mouth toward the breast. Bring your baby's head in toward your breast by moving the bent arm in (don't lean into the baby; it may make your back ache).

In this position, you hold the baby's neck and the back of your baby's head in the hand that is opposite to the breast being used, while the baby's body lies across your body. If your baby is nursing at the left breast, your right hand will be holding the baby's head and the baby's feet will be on your right side. Put the baby's face in front of your breast and use your free hand to hold your breast. Put your thumb slightly to the side, a little more than an inch from your nipple, and your index finger opposite the thumb. Touch your baby's lip or the side of the mouth with the nipple so that he or she will open the mouth toward the breast. Then move the baby's head in toward you, until he or she begins to suck.

Crossover Hold

Football Hold

The football hold keeps the baby's weight off your abdomen, so it can be especially good after a caesarean birth. With your baby facing you, hold his or her whole body, including the back of the neck and head, with the hand on the same side as the breast being used. If your baby is nursing from the left breast, your left hand should hold the baby, while the baby's bottom goes against the bed or chair you are sitting on, and the baby's feet are toward the back of the bed or chair. Use the opposite hand to lift the breast, with the thumb on top of the nipple and the index finger below. Touch your baby's lip with the nipple so that he or she will open the mouth toward the breast. Then move the baby's head in toward you, until he or she begins to suck.

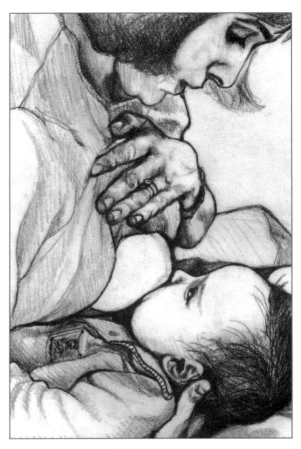

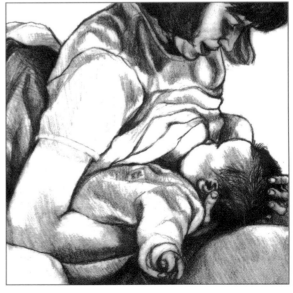

Side-Lying Position

Lying on your side, place your baby on the side also, so that the baby's face is toward your breast. If you are on your left side, your baby will be on his or her right side. Bring your left arm straight down under the baby, holding him or her close to you. You might need to put a pillow under your baby to make this more comfortable for both of you. Use your opposite hand to lift the breast, with the thumb on top of the nipple and the index finger below. Touch your baby's lip with the nipple so that he or she will open the mouth toward the breast. Then move the baby's head in toward you, until he or she begins to suck.

Breastfeeding twins

If you have twins, you may sometimes nurse both of them at the same time. You can do this most easily with the football hold, the cradle hold, or a combination of the two. The hardest part of nursing two babies at once is getting each one started nursing on a breast. You may need help in the early weeks.

HOW MUCH TO NURSE YOUR BABY

Especially at first, your baby will be in charge of how often you nurse, and for how long. As your baby grows, you can begin to shift feedings so that they fit better in your lifestyle—and so that you can get more sleep—but it's still important to pay attention to how often your baby seems to want to nurse.

Newborns nurse from 8 to 12 times a day, or every 1 1/2 to 3 hours. It is important to feed your baby whenever he or she wants to eat ("on-demand" feeding) so that you can build up your milk supply for future feedings.

As your baby grows and your milk supply is established, your baby will take in more milk at each feeding, and the feedings will begin to be further apart.

By about 6 weeks, your baby is likely to be nursing every 2 to 3 hours, with a longer period between feedings at night. (If your baby has a longer period between feedings during the day than at night, you may want to wake him or her to take another feeding during the day. After a while, this will change the feeding schedule.)

When your baby weighs 12 pounds or more, he or she probably will sleep "through the night." With a new baby, this means 5 or 6 hours.

Your baby probably will nurse for about 20 minutes on each breast during a feeding. At first, a newborn may fall asleep while nursing, then wake and suck some more. Your baby may not be finished, even if he or she is dozing a little.

Always allow the baby to finish the first breast. When the baby spits out the nipple, burp him or her and then offer the second breast. Some babies fill up on one side. This is perfectly normal. At the next feeding, start with the breast the baby did not nurse from.

As your baby gets older, he or she is likely to nurse more actively and feedings may get slightly shorter. Sometimes your baby may continue to suck, even when it seems like there's almost no milk left in your breast. This sucking doesn't mean

How often should I nurse my baby?

that the baby is still hungry. It is a way for your baby to satisfy a natural sucking need.

Years ago, nursing mothers were advised to nurse no more than a few minutes on each breast, in order to prevent cracked or sore nipples. Today it's believed that longer feeding sessions do not cause sore nipples.

Average Intake Guidelines by Age

0 - 2 MONTHS	2 - 5 ounces per feeding
2 - 4 MONTHS	3 - 6 ounces per feeding
4 - 6 MONTHS	4 - 7 ounces per feeding

Use these average amounts as guidelines for how much your baby should be feeding once feedings are established at about three weeks of age.

BURPING YOUR BABY

Babies swallow some air while they are nursing. This can make them uncomfortable, so you should help your baby burp swallowed air out after each feeding and when you change breasts during a feeding.

The most common burping position is holding the baby to the shoulder as you pat his or her back. You may find this is the most natural and comfortable position for you, and it is the least likely to cause milk to "urp" out. There are other positions you can try as well:

- Sit the baby on your lap, facing outward. Support your baby's head with one hand just under the jaw while you gently pat or rub your baby on the lower back.
- Rest your baby on his or her stomach, across your knees, and pat or rub your baby's back.

Your baby may burp up some milk along with air. This is nothing to worry about, but it means you should protect your clothing by putting a clean cloth diaper or a towel under your baby's mouth before burping.

If your baby vomits what seems like a whole feeding, rather than just spitting up a little milk, it may be that something you ate disagreed with your baby's digestion. If it happens more than once, you should call your health care provider, especially if your baby also has a fever.

You can burp a baby by sitting him or her on your lap, facing out, then rubbing or patting the baby on the back.

BOWEL MOVEMENTS

Your baby's bowel movements during the first few days after birth will be black, tarry, and loose. These first bowel movements are called **meconium**.

As the colostrum your breasts are producing becomes milk, your baby's bowel movements will change.

Breastfed babies normally have yellowish, very loose bowel movements, at least once a day.

After the first few days, a baby that is nursing well will have at least six wet diapers and one bowel movement every day.

The log on the following pages can help you tell if your baby is off to a good start nursing. If something puzzles you, or if your baby isn't having as many bowel movements or wet diapers as described above, talk it over with a lactation consultant or your health care provider.

FIRST WEEK DAILY BREASTFEEDING LOG

Circle the hour when your baby nurses. Put a "B" above the hour of day if your baby nursed both breasts. If one breast only, place "L" for left breast or "R" for right breast. Circle the W when your baby has a wet diaper. Circle the S when your baby has a soiled diaper. It would be best to use cloth diapers or inexpensive disposable diapers the first week of your baby's life. This makes it easier for you to tell if your baby has urinated.

Birthdate:____/____/____   Time:_____ AM PM

DAY ONE:
Breastfeeding Time:
12 1 2 3 4 5 6 7 8 9 10 11 12 1 2 3 4 5 6 7 8 9 10 11
GOAL: 8 to 12 times per day
Audible swallowing: yes   no
Wet diaper: W
Black tarry soiled diaper: S

DAY TWO:
Breastfeeding Time:
12 1 2 3 4 5 6 7 8 9 10 11 12 1 2 3 4 5 6 7 8 9 10 11
GOAL: 8 to 12 times per day
Audible swallowing: yes   no
Wet diaper: W   W
Black tarry soiled diaper: S   S

DAY THREE:
Breastfeeding Time:
12 1 2 3 4 5 6 7 8 9 10 11 12 1 2 3 4 5 6 7 8 9 10 11
GOAL: 8 to 12 times per day
Audible swallowing: yes   no
Wet diaper: W   W   W
Green soiled diaper: S   S

DAY FOUR:

Breastfeeding Time:

12 1 2 3 4 5 6 7 8 9 10 11 12 1 2 3 4 5 6 7 8 9 10 11

GOAL: 8 to 12 times per day

Audible swallowing: yes   no

Wet diaper: W   W   W   W

Yellow soiled diaper: S   S   S

DAY FIVE:

Breastfeeding Time:

12 1 2 3 4 5 6 7 8 9 10 11 12 1 2 3 4 5 6 7 8 9 10 11

GOAL: 8 to 12 times per day

Audible swallowing: yes   no

Wet diaper: W   W   W   W

Yellow soiled diaper: S   S   S

DAY SIX:

Breastfeeding Time:

12 1 2 3 4 5 6 7 8 9 10 11 12 1 2 3 4 5 6 7 8 9 10 11

GOAL: 8 to 12 times per day

Audible swallowing: yes   no

Wet diaper: W   W   W   W

Yellow soiled diaper: S   S   S   S

DAY SEVEN:

Breastfeeding Time:

12 1 2 3 4 5 6 7 8 9 10 11 12 1 2 3 4 5 6 7 8 9 10 11

GOAL: 8 to 12 times per day

Audible swallowing: yes   no

Wet diaper: W   W   W   W   W   W

Yellow soiled diaper: S   S   S   S

If your baby is not breastfeeding 8 to 12 times a day or seems to be breastfeeding all the time, or if your baby has *fewer* wet or soiled diapers than the number on the log, call your baby's health care provider.

FEEDING THE OCCASIONAL BOTTLE

BREASTFEEDING alone is best for the first 3 or 4 weeks after your baby is born. It helps your milk supply come in, and it helps your baby develop a strong nursing pattern. The longer you can keep giving your baby only the breast, the easier the nursing "rhythm" between the two of you will be.

But you may be going back to work, or at least needing an occasional time away from your baby. Your baby can take a bottle during these times, and you can continue breastfeeding as well.

The best nutrition for your baby comes from your breast milk. Even if you give your baby an occasional bottle, it's best if you express breast milk and save it, rather than using prepared formula.

EXPRESSING MILK

You can express milk by hand in this way: Circle your breast firmly with your fingers about an inch and a half back from the nipple. Push back towards your chest, then squeeze forward and lift the nipple. (Yes, it looks something like milking a cow.)

There are a variety of pumps available, from simple hand-operated ones to expensive electric machines. If you only need to express milk occasionally, a hand pump probably will do just fine. If you are going back to work and will be away from your baby quite a bit, it is best to buy or rent an electric pump that allows you to express more milk quickly.

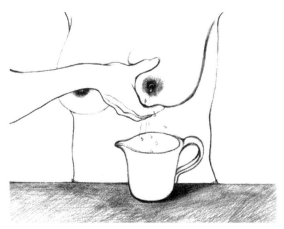

Even if you can't be there for a feeding, you can express and save breast milk for your baby.

STORING MILK

You can store breast milk for as long as 6 months in your refrigerator's freezer, and up to 3 days in the main part of the refrigerator. Breast milk can be stored in bottles or plastic bottle liners. The following chart shows guidelines for storage.

Breast Milk Storage Guidelines				
	Room Temperature	Refrigerator	Refrigerator Freezer	Deep Freezer
Freshly Expressed Breast Milk	6 -10 hours	72 hours	6 months	12 months
Thawed Breast Milk (previously frozen)	Do not store	24 hours	Never refreeze thawed milk	Never refreeze thawed milk

USING A BOTTLE

There are several kinds of bottles and nipples available. If you are breastfeeding, it's helpful to use a nipple that makes sucking from a bottle similar to nursing from a breast.

A regular nipple is easy for babies to use because it allows a generous flow of milk, but this can make nursing at the breast harder for the baby.

What if I want to bottlefeed my baby?

If you occasionally feed your baby from a bottle, use a nipple like the Avent or Johnson Healthflow. These nipples will make it less likely that your baby will start to prefer the bottle over the breast.

Other tips for giving an occasional bottle:

- *Many babies will take a bottle more easily from someone other than their mother, whom they associate with nursing.*
- *You, or whoever is feeding your baby, should give the bottle in a different place than where you normally nurse.*
- *Give a bottle between feedings, rather than replacing a feeding, if this is possible.*

There are a number of nipples available, including the Healthflow (left) and the Avent (right).

BREASTFEEDING PROBLEMS

BREASTFEEDING is a natural, healthy process. Most women are able to breastfeed successfully almost without thinking about it. But for some women, there may be occasional problems.

Try not to give up breastfeeding if you have a problem. A lactation consultant or your health care provider can help you figure out how to breastfeed successfully.

Some common problems are:

ENGORGEMENT

With engorged breasts, you may feel like you have two large, hard, painful balls resting on your chest, rather than the soft breasts you are used to. As your milk supply grows, the milk, blood, and fluid in your breasts can build up to a point where the breasts are so hard and full that it's difficult for your baby to nurse. Frequent nursing from birth can prevent engorgement. Make sure you are nursing from both breasts every couple of hours during the first week—even if you have to wake your baby to do it. Massage can help relieve engorgement by stimulating the let-down of milk. Some women find that putting a warm compress on the breast a few minutes before nursing will help with let-down. Ice can also be used to reduce inflammation and swelling.

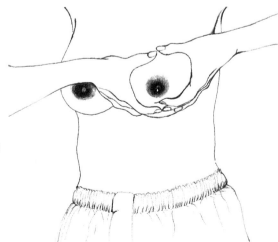

Gently massaging your breast with both hands can help relieve engorgement.

LET-DOWN DIFFICULTIES

In the first few days of breastfeeding, you may not feel your milk "letting down" into the breast. Try to stay relaxed—being anxious can cause some difficulty with let-down—and nurse your baby regularly (every 2 or 3 hours) during the first week after birth. Make sure that your baby has the nipple fully in his or her mouth.

LEAKING NIPPLES

Some women find the let-down reflex so powerful, once they've been nursing for a week or so, that the sound of someone else's baby crying can cause milk to begin leaking from their breasts. This will become less of a problem with time. To handle leaking, use nursing pads in your bra—and carry extras. When you first feel a tingling, press your arms against the nipple and squeeze yourself to prevent leaking.

SORE NIPPLES

Why do I have sore nipples?

Sore, cracked nipples can be a small irritation or a major problem for the nursing mother. Often they are caused by the baby not nursing properly, so that the tip of your nipple is getting most of the sucking, rather than most or all of the areola. Some suggestions for preventing or minimizing sore nipples:

- Manually express a little milk before giving the baby your breast, in order to get more of the areola in your baby's mouth.
- Make sure your baby's mouth is wide open, with the lips in a "flanged" position, or puckered like a fish. Put the nipple as far into the baby's mouth as you can.
- When nursing on a breast is finished, do not pull your breast from the baby's closed mouth; instead, loosen the baby's mouth by putting a finger gently between the baby's gums.
- Dry your nipples after a feeding by keeping them uncovered for 15 to 20 minutes.
- Don't use soap on your nipples. Special glands secrete a lubricant that helps protect the nipple and areole. If you use soap, this lubricant will be washed away and your nipples will be too dry. Wash your nipples with plain warm water.

- Rub breast milk over your nipples, or use a lanolin-based cream to lubricate them.
- If your nipples remain sore, or are so painful that you don't want to nurse, talk to a lactation consultant or your health care provider.

BREAST INFECTION

Soreness in the breast (usually only one is affected, but it is possible for both to be infected), along with cold- and flu-like symptoms—chills, achiness, vomiting, a temperature over 100.4°—may mean an infection. A breast infection can be caused by a plugged milk duct or by bacteria entering through a cracked nipple. If you think you have a breast infection, you need to see your health care provider as quickly as possible for diagnosis and treatment with antibiotics. Remind your health care provider that you are breastfeeding so he or she can pre-scribe medication that will not affect nursing.

MILK SUPPLY

You will probably worry more than you need to about whether your body is making enough milk. The more your baby nurses, and the more your baby takes during each feeding, the more your body will produce. Unless your health care provider or a lactation consultant advises it, you should not begin feeding your baby formula in order to make sure he or she is getting enough milk. That only makes the problem (if there is a prob-lem) worse: The more you feed something other than breast milk, the less breast milk you will produce and so the more you will need to feed something other than breast milk.

BABY REFUSES OR PULLS AWAY FROM THE BREAST

Sometimes your baby will stop in the middle of a feeding, even though he or she doesn't seem to have taken enough milk. Or, as your baby grows older, he or she may turn away from the breast altogether. There are a number of possible reasons for pulling away or refusing the breast:

- **Your baby may have a cold, and may find it hard to breathe while nursing.** Or having a cold may just make your baby cranky and fussy. Breastfeeding helps to clear the congestion.

What if my baby won't take the breast?

- **Your baby may need to be burped.** Air in the tummy is making it uncomfortable to nurse.
- **Milk may be coming out so quickly at first that your baby can't swallow it fast enough.** Express a little milk before nursing to lessen the flow. This problem will disappear as your baby grows.
- **Your baby may have a yeast infection, called "thrush," which makes nursing painful.** Call your health care provider if you see a whitish coating in your baby's mouth.

TIREDNESS, DEPRESSION

Your body uses more energy than you realize to produce milk while you are breastfeeding. Be sure to eat when you are hungry to keep your energy level up. If you expected to bounce back to pre-pregnancy energy once your baby was born, you may be surprised to find how quickly you tire and how much sleep you seem to need. This is normal after having a baby.

Treat yourself well. Rest, exercise regularly, and eat good food. Ask for help, and don't try to do too much too quickly.

If the fatigue seems overwhelming, talk to your health care provider.

BOTTLEFEEDING

BREAST MILK is the best food for most babies, but prepared infant formulas have been developed that are the next best thing to mother's milk.

Babies less than a year old should be fed iron-fortified formula, not regular cow's milk. Talk with your baby's health care provider about what kind of formula will be best.

Concentrated liquid or powdered formulas need to be mixed with water. Use the water from your sink, so your baby will get enough fluoride and other minerals. If you have well water, have the water tested by a certified lab to ensure that it is safe to drink, has sufficient fluoride, and contains no nitrates. If you choose to mix concentrated liquid or powdered formula with bottled water, find out the source and quality of the water first (much bottled water comes from wells). Like well water, bottled water must contain fluoride—a necessary nutrient—and be free of nitrates.

There are several varieties of bottles and nipples available. A regular nipple gives an ample supply of milk and is easy for a baby to suck. Sometimes finding the "right" nipple is a trial-and-error process, and what's right for your baby may be different than what was right for your sister's baby or your neighbor's baby.

PREPARING FORMULA

- **Use fresh formula.** Don't use formula after the date stamped on it. Store any opened formula you don't use in the refrigerator, and throw it away after 48 hours. What formula the baby does not drink from its bottle should be thrown away.
- **Clean bottles thoroughly between feedings.** Use hot, clean soapy water to wash bottles, nipples, and rings. A bottle brush should be used to scrub the inside of the bottle and the nipple. Rinse everything well.
- **You can feed your baby at any safe temperature, without worrying about heating to the "right" temperature.** Some babies will drink formula straight from the refrigerator. Others prefer their formula warmed. An easy way to warm formula is simply to hold it under warm running tap water,

How long can I keep formula?

or to place it in a bowl of warm water for a few minutes. *Never* heat formula in a microwave oven. Test the warmth of the formula on the inside of your wrist.

- **When using concentrated liquid formula:**
  - Clean the top of the can and then shake it before opening.
  - Use a measuring cup and put equal amounts of tap water and liquid formula into a clean bottle, water first. For example, to mix 4 ounces of formula, put 2 ounces of tap water in a bottle, then 2 ounces of concentrated liquid formula. Put a clean nipple on the bottle, then shake to mix the formula and water. Test the temperature of the mixed formula on your wrist to make sure it's not too hot, then feed your baby. Throw away any formula in the bottle you don't use during this feeding.
- **When mixing powdered formula:**

  Use one scoop of powdered formula (the scoop comes with the powdered formula) for every 2 ounces of tap water. For example, to mix 4 ounces of formula, you would put 4 ounces of tap water in the bottle, then 2 scoops of powdered formula.

Never try to "stretch" formula, whether liquid or powdered, by adding more water than the directions call for. If you are having trouble finding the money to buy formula, ask your health care provider for information on obtaining assistance through the Women, Infant, and Children (WIC) program administered by the federal government.

FEEDING YOUR BABY A BOTTLE

When you're rushed and tired, you may just want to prop up a bottle in your baby's mouth to feed while you do other things. This is a bad idea for you and your baby because:

- It can be dangerous. Your baby can choke, or develop ear infections.
- It can cause tooth decay. The formula (or any other sweet liquid, including breast milk) will puddle in your baby's mouth, if he or she goes to sleep with a bottle. The natural sugar in the liquid will form an acid that damages the baby's teeth.

- It can hurt your baby's emotional development. Babies need to be touched and held. Feeding is a natural time to cuddle your baby in a relaxed way, whether you are breastfeeding or using a bottle. The best thing you can do for your baby is to sit quietly in a calm place while feeding your baby.

GETTING STARTED

The log on the following pages will help you keep track of how much formula your baby is taking and whether he or she is having regular wet and soiled diapers.

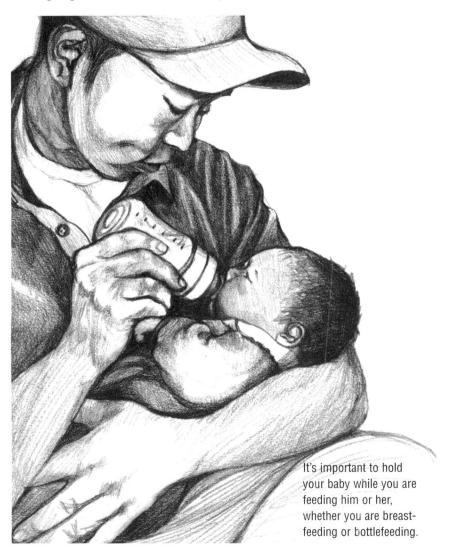

It's important to hold your baby while you are feeding him or her, whether you are breast-feeding or bottlefeeding.

FIRST WEEK DAILY BOTTLEFEEDING LOG
Circle the hour your baby eats. Circle the W when your baby has a wet diaper. Circle the S when your baby has a soiled diaper. It would be best to use cloth diapers or inexpensive disposable diapers the first week of your baby's life. This makes it easier for you to tell if your baby has urinated.

Birthdate:____/____/____   Time:_____ AM PM

DAY ONE:
Bottlefeeding Time:
12 1 2 3 4 5 6 7 8 9 10 11 12 1 2 3 4 5 6 7 8 9 10 11
GOAL: 6 to 12 times per day
Audible swallowing: yes   no
Wet diaper: W
Black tarry soiled diaper: S

DAY TWO:
Bottlefeeding Time:
12 1 2 3 4 5 6 7 8 9 10 11 12 1 2 3 4 5 6 7 8 9 10 11
GOAL: 6 to 12 times per day
Audible swallowing: yes   no
Wet diaper: W   W
Black tarry soiled diaper: S   S

DAY THREE:
Bottlefeeding Time:
12 1 2 3 4 5 6 7 8 9 10 11 12 1 2 3 4 5 6 7 8 9 10 11
GOAL: 6 to 12 times per day
Audible swallowing: yes   no
Wet diaper: W   W   W
Green soiled diaper: S   S

DAY FOUR:
Bottlefeeding Time:

12 1 2 3 4 5 6 7 8 9 10 11 12 1 2 3 4 5 6 7 8 9 10 11

GOAL: 6 to 12 times per day

Audible swallowing: yes   no

Wet diaper: W W W W

Yellow soiled diaper: S S

DAY FIVE:
Bottlefeeding Time:

12 1 2 3 4 5 6 7 8 9 10 11 12 1 2 3 4 5 6 7 8 9 10 11

GOAL: 6 to 12 times per day

Audible swallowing: yes   no

Wet diaper: W W W W

Yellow soiled diaper: S S S

DAY SIX:
Bottlefeeding Time:

12 1 2 3 4 5 6 7 8 9 10 11 12 1 2 3 4 5 6 7 8 9 10 11

GOAL: 6 to 12 times per day

Audible swallowing: yes   no

Wet diaper: W W W W

Yellow soiled diaper: S S S

DAY SEVEN:
Bottlefeeding Time:

12 1 2 3 4 5 6 7 8 9 10 11 12 1 2 3 4 5 6 7 8 9 10 11

GOAL: 6 to 12 times per day

Audible swallowing: yes   no

Wet diaper: W W W W W W

Yellow soiled diaper: S S S

If your baby is not eating 6 to 12 times a day or seems to be eating all the time, or if your baby has *fewer* wet or soiled diapers than the number on the log, call your baby's health care provider.

FOR PARTNERS

IF THE BABY'S mother is breastfeeding, you may think there's not much you can do now. For some partners, that's a relief (you don't have to be the one to get up in the middle of the night), and, for others, it feels like you're missing out on something special.

While it's true you can't nurse the baby, you can both help your partner nurse and take part in the special bonding.

Some partners help the nursing mother by being the one to pick up the crying baby in the middle of the night, changing the diaper, and then bringing the baby to the mother for nursing. This helps the nursing mother get a little more needed sleep.

You can burp the baby after nursing, maybe rocking or walking around holding the baby.

You may be a bit jealous, or upset, by seeing your partner's breasts in a completely different way than you're used to. Or you may be somewhat aroused. These are all normal feelings. It may help to talk about them with your partner or someone else.

FOR MORE INFORMATION

Nursing Mother, Working Mother by Gayle Pryor.
The Nursing Mother's Companion by Kathleen Huggins, RN, MS.
The Womanly Art of Breastfeeding by La Leche League.

Your Baby's First 15 Months

You wondered what your baby would be like, and now the baby is here, a separate person who needs a lot from you.

The first fifteen months of your baby's life are important for physical, mental, and emotional development. You want to take care of your baby the best way you can, whether that means getting the proper immunizations or playing games that will help your baby's development.

The first 15 months are a busy time for parents as their baby changes from a helpless newborn to a little person who walks and talks and shows you an independent personality.

SOME OF THE QUESTIONS ANSWERED IN THIS CHAPTER INCLUDE:

- What makes a good parent?
- What changes will I see in my baby?
- How do I keep my baby safe?
- How can I help my baby develop?
- What immunizations will my baby need?
- When will my baby start eating solid food?
- When will my baby start to walk?

BECOMING A PARENT

A THREE-YEAR-OLD girl is told that her mommy is going to have a new baby and that she "is going to be a big sister." She looks forward to it for months. Then the new baby is born and the three-year-old is very upset. "You said I was going to be a *big* sister," she cries. "But I'm still the same size!"

When you have your first baby, you may feel a lot like that three-year-old. Now you have a baby, but you're still the same person. What does it take to be a *parent*?

We have to learn how to be parents the same way we learn most things: by getting information, by watching others, by doing.

What makes a good parent?

- **Getting information**

    While you were pregnant, you may have read books about pregnancy, childbirth, and babies. There are dozens of books about children and parenting available (see the list of resources at the end of this chapter, for example). Numerous videos and audiotapes are also available. In most communities there are groups devoted to supporting and educating parents. One such group is the La Leche League, which has chapters everywhere in the United States, and not only helps new mothers breastfeed, but also offers opportunities for sharing parenting information and concerns with other mothers. Check with your health care provider for information about other groups in your community.

- **Watching others**

    The example for raising children that has probably had the most influence on you is that set by your own parents. But now that you have your own baby, you need to stop and think about what kind of parents you had and what parts of their parenting style you want to keep—and what parts you don't.

    Your mother may have been wonderful at changing your diapers and keeping you fed and clean, but perhaps she was uncomfortable showing emotion, so she didn't kiss or hug you often. Or she may have been affectionate and warm, but missed appointments at the clinic and rarely cooked a meal.

Think about your friends and other relatives. What do you see about the way they raise their children that you like? What do you see that you don't like? Whose children seem happy and loved? Don't be afraid to ask others about their ideas on being a parent—and don't be afraid to ignore any ideas that don't seem right to you.

Decide what your priorities are—and what's best for your child. No parent is perfect, but we all want to be the best parent we can be.

- **Doing**

No matter how much you've read about being a parent or watched other parents, you will learn most about how to be a parent simply by *being* one.

If you don't know how to change a diaper, the nurses at the hospital will teach you before you go home. But you will only become good at changing diapers after you've changed a few by yourself.

If you're nervous about breastfeeding, your health care provider and a lactation specialist will help you get started. But it's only by doing it that you will find the position that works best for you and your baby.

Because you will pay attention to your own child, you will learn the difference between your baby's tired cry and your baby's hungry cry. You will learn that your child is uneasy around other people and needs to be held when visitors are around—or you'll learn that your child loves the attention of other people and may need a little control in order not to become too excited.

The Most Important Person in Your Baby's Life Is You

A child's first important connection is with his or her parents. It's a connection that starts even before the baby is born. Recent studies show that babies can hear while they are still in the womb, and that they remember what they hear in some way. Since the sound they will hear most often is the mother's voice, a newborn baby responds more to the mother's voice than to the voice of anyone else.

In some cultures, babies are strapped to their mothers' backs or chests for most of the day and night during the first months after birth. This practice is uncommon in the United States, but American babies still need to sense the warmth, sounds, and smells of the mother. The more you hold your baby and talk to your baby and play with your baby, the better.

Being a parent is not a part-time job. It's a lot of hard work—and it's a lot of fun. There is nothing that can make you happier than watching your baby's face when you walk into a room.

Even if you work outside the home, you are still a full-time parent. Other people may take care of your baby while you're at work, but you are still the most important person in your baby's life. Although you may be tired when you get home, you need to make sure your child doesn't miss your attention. Now is the time to pick up your baby or toddler, cuddle, sing a song, or read a story. Show your love. It's a good way for you to relax after work, and it's something your baby needs.

PARENTING PROBLEMS

If you feel overwhelmed, tell someone. Your health care provider can help direct you to services or counselors when you think you just can't handle your child or being a parent. Being a parent *is* hard, even when everything is fine. If you have a colicky baby who cries all the time, or a toddler who seems out of control, parenting can seem impossible.

Don't be embarrassed to admit that you don't think you can handle the situation. Most parents have felt that way at one time or another. Sometimes a little reassurance is all you need to feel more confident.

Whatever you do, *never* take your frustration out on your child. If you feel in danger of losing control, get help immediately. Find someone to look after your child for an hour or two while you do what you need to calm down, whether that involves taking a nap, walking around the block, or talking to a friend or relative.

It is especially important that you never shake your baby. Shaking can cause permanent brain damage, even death. Make it clear to your daycare providers and babysitters that they should never shake your baby either, for any reason.

You and your baby share a special connection. Spend time looking into your baby's face, talking, and showing different expressions.

YOUR BABY: 2 WEEKS TO 2 MONTHS

DURING THE FIRST 2 months of your baby's life, you will see big changes in the way your baby looks, acts, and even "talks" to you. From a newborn who doesn't seem to do much more than eat, sleep, and cry, your baby will grow very quickly into a little person who smiles and coos and examines the world.

NUTRITION

- The only food your baby needs right now is breast milk or iron-fortified formula. Do not try to introduce any other foods when your baby is this young; the baby's digestive system is not ready to handle them.
- You will be feeding your baby every 2 to 4 hours, although the schedule is likely to change from day to day.
- The more often your baby eats during the day, the more likely the baby will sleep for a longer stretch (5 to 8 hours) at night.

ELIMINATION

- Breastfed babies usually have small, seedy, yellowish or golden stools—and they have them fairly often, especially for the first 7 weeks. As the baby gets older, there should be fewer stools each day.
- Babies that are fed formula have 1 to 4 stools a day. These stools should be soft, and the color will vary depending on the type of formula used.
- You will learn to recognize your baby's normal stools. Watch for any big change in the color, frequency, or texture of your baby's stools. It can be a sign of allergy (to formula or to something you may have eaten that is passed on through breast milk), or of illness.
- Your baby should have 6 to 8 wet diapers every day, with small amounts of urine each time.

SLEEP

- Babies at this age sleep from 16 to 20 hours a day. Your baby's sleep pattern will vary from day to day.
- If your baby sleeps longer than 3 1/2 to 4 hours during the day, wake the baby for a feeding. You want to save the longer sleep periods for night, when you can sleep, too.

- When you feed your baby at night, do it with a little more peace and quiet than during the day, so the baby will go back to sleep, rather than think it's playtime.
- Babies should be put to sleep on their backs or sides, *not* on their tummies. Tummy-sleeping has been found to be associated with Sudden Infant Death Syndrome (SIDS).
- The best place for your baby to sleep is on a firm mattress in a crib. There is no harm in putting your baby in his or her own room at night.
- Your baby probably will start to sleep "through the night" (7 to 8 hours) when he or she weighs about 12 pounds or is about 2 months old.
- If you start a sleep routine, even with a newborn, it will help the baby learn when to sleep as he or she grows. The routine might be cleaning the baby with a washcloth, putting on a fresh diaper and clean clothes, feeding the baby, burping, then rocking or sitting with the baby in a quiet and dark or dimly-lit room until the baby falls asleep.

GROWTH AND DEVELOPMENT

- Your baby can hear from the moment of birth. You can see your baby react to sounds by blinking, crying, getting quiet, or startling (a jerky motion). Your baby knows the sound of your voice at birth, and will keep learning and responding to your voice.
- A newborn can see about about a foot away. By the time your baby is 2 months old, he or she will be able to see things about 10 feet away. At about 6 weeks old, your baby should start to follow things—especially you—with his or her eyes, and to smile back at you when you are smiling.
- At about 2 to 3 weeks, your baby may have a period of crying, usually in the early evening. This is a normal fussy period, but it is sometimes hard on parents because it may seem like nothing you do helps calm your baby. Try to soothe your baby by rocking, walking, or patting him or her on the back. It's okay to let your baby cry for about 15 minutes and then try to soothe the baby again. Keep this up

What changes will I see in my baby?

until the crying stops—the entire process can take as long as 2 to 3 hours. Babies eventually outgrow this fussiness.

- True colic starts earlier than 2 to 3 weeks and is more severe and unpredictable than evening fussiness. If your baby seems to have colic, call your health care provider.

SOCIAL

- At first your baby will be quiet—often sleeping—when comfortable and fed, and will cry when uncomfortable or hungry.

- As the baby develops, he or she will begin to smile at people, usually the mother first and then the father, brothers and sisters, daycare providers, and others who are around often and are part of the baby's life.

- By the time your baby is 2 months old, he or she will show excitement—moving arms and legs, making noises, smiling—and will be able to calm himself or herself by sucking on fingers or a pacifier.

- Your baby will show that he or she likes to be with people, staying awake longer when people are around and even "showing off" for others.

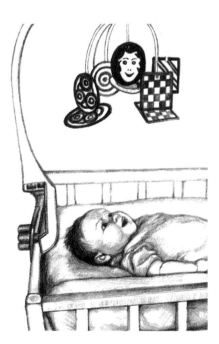

Mobiles and other bright objects or pictures will attract your baby's attention and interest.

How do I keep my baby safe?

How can I help my baby develop?

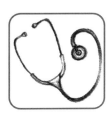

What immunizations will my baby need?

SAFETY

- Always use an approved car seat, and place it facing the rear, preferably in the middle of the back seat.
- Never leave your baby alone on a high place or in bath water, not even for a quick moment. Babies can roll off a dressing table or sink under the water in seconds.
- Always hold your baby when feeding a bottle. Leaving a bottle propped up so your baby can feed without you being there can cause choking, and has been found to increase ear infections.

ACTIVITIES TO HELP YOUR BABY'S DEVELOPMENT

- Put your baby on his or her stomach on a flat surface and then talk, show toys, or hold up a mirror to encourage your baby to try to lift his or her head and, thereby, strengthen the shoulder and neck muscles. (Don't leave your baby on his or her stomach to fall asleep.)
- Hold your baby in a sitting position in your lap, facing you. Hold your baby's shoulders forward, giving more support. From this position, your baby can see what's going on around him or her and can look into your eyes.
- Put your baby on his or her back and encourage arm and foot movement by putting brightly colored or noise-making toys on a foot or hand.

CLINIC VISITS

AFTER YOUR FIRST clinic visit with your new baby, your health care provider will establish a schedule for health exams. The times you see the health care provider are usually planned to coincide with the schedule for immunizations.

You may see your health care provider during your baby's first 2 months if your baby is ill with a cold or ear infection. The tiny body of your baby can get very sick quickly, so don't wait to talk with your health care provider if your baby seems sick.

The immunizations given during the first 2 months are:

- **Hepatitis B.** This prevents infection of the liver that can be caused by the Hepatitis B virus. The first shot of this vaccine is usually given between 2 weeks and 2 months, and the second shot between 2 months and 4 months.

- **DTP or DTAP.** This combination immunization protects against diphtheria, pertussis (or whooping cough), and tetanus. The first shot is given at 2 months.
- **Polio.** The polio vaccine can be given as either an oral solution or an injection. Polio can paralyze or kill, but because of the vaccine, it is far less common today than it was forty to fifty years ago.
- **Hib.** This vaccine protects against the Haemophilus Influenzae Type B bacteria, which can cause brain damage, pneumonia, infection, and even death in young children. The vaccine is given in a shot, starting at 2 months.

At your baby's 2-month clinic visit, he or she will get 3 or 4 immunizations, depending on the current medical recommendations. Most babies cry when they get shots, but their discomfort is very brief.

Non-Prescription Pain and Fever Medication

Your baby is likely to get a number of colds and viruses during his or her first 15 months, and your health care provider may recommend that you give your baby an over-the-counter medication like Tylenol or Advil to help control the fever and ease his or her aches and pains. (You should not give medications, especially aspirin, to your baby without the advice of your health care provider.) The chart below shows the correct dosages for your baby as he or she grows and gains weight.

	ACETAMINOPHEN (Tylenol, Tempra)		IBUPROFEN (Motrin, Advil, Pediaprofen)	
WEIGHT IN POUNDS	INFANT DROPS 80 mg/0.8 ml	ELIXIR/SUSPENSION 160 mg/5 ml	INFANT DROPS 50 mg/1.25 ml	Suspension 100 mg/5 ml
12–14	0.8 ml	1/2 tsp	1.25 ml	1/2 tsp
15–17	1.0 ml	2/3 tsp	2.0 ml	3/4 tsp
18–22	1.2 ml	3/4 tsp	2.5 ml	1 tsp
23–29	1.6 ml	1 tsp	3.25 ml	11/4 tsp
30–34	2.0 ml	11/4 tsp	3.75 ml	11/2 tsp
35–40	2.4 ml	11/2 tsp	–	13/4 tsp
41–46	–	13/4 tsp	–	2 tsp
47–52	–	2 tsp	–	21/2 tsp

A few times a day, put your baby on his or her tummy and show toys or other interesting things. This will encourage your baby to lift his or her head and strengthen the neck and spine.

YOUR BABY: 2 MONTHS TO 4 MONTHS

THIS CAN BE an easy-going time. Your baby cries less—the early-evening fussy period usually disappears by 3 months—and sleeps more. Your baby is more interested in the world and in othe people, and is easier to take places with you. Routines are becoming established, with more regular times for eating, sleeping, and playing.

Your tiredness and feelings of frustration are likely to be over as well. When you look at this happy little baby who smiles every time you come into the room, you forget that there may have been some difficult times during the first 2 months.

NUTRITION

- Breast milk or iron-fortified formula is still the best nourishment for your baby, and other foods should not be introduced yet. If you think your baby needs cereal or other solids, talk about it with your health care provider before you feed them to your baby.
- Your baby will breastfeed about 6 times a day.
- If you are feeding your baby formula, he or she should take 20 to 32 ounces of formula a day.
- Your baby will take most feedings during the day and sleep longer at night.

ELIMINATION

- Breastfed babies may have stools several times a day or as seldom as once a week. Either, or any number in between, is normal if it is a regular pattern for your baby.
- Formula-fed babies usually have from 1 stool every few days to 4 a day. These stools are soft.
- Most infants urinate often, in small amounts. Your baby should have several wet diapers each day.

SLEEP

- Most babies begin to sleep longer at night—7 to 8 hours. They may then wake up for a feeding and fall back asleep for another 3 to 4 hours. (Which means you get more sleep now, too.)

- Naps during the day can vary. Your baby may take one short nap, one long nap, or none at all. Or your baby may take several naps.
- You can help your baby learn how to go to sleep on his or her own now. When you notice your baby getting tired, try putting him or her in the crib while still awake, so he or she can learn how to go from being awake to being asleep.
- Give the last feeding about half an hour to an hour before putting your baby into the crib for the night, so your baby learns to separate the idea of eating from sleeping.

GROWTH AND DEVELOPMENT

What changes will I see in my baby?

- Your baby's vision is now like that of an adult, and the eye adjusts to objects at different distances.
- Your baby will play with his or her fingers.
- Your baby begins to reach for and grab things, although still clumsily. Your baby may be able to bear weight on his or her feet, and to lift the chest up when placed on his or her tummy.
- Drooling starts at about 3 months, although teething doesn't usually start until 6 to 10 months.
- Your baby learns by putting things in his or her mouth, starting with his or her own fingers and then anything else in reach.

SOCIAL

- Your baby smiles, coos, and responds to people—especially you. By the fourth month, your baby may be able to have a whole "conversation," babbling and cooing sounds in a string. In a good mood, your baby may squeal, giggle, laugh, and grin for as long as 30 minutes.
- If people are around to socialize with your baby, he or she will play twice as long as when alone.

SAFETY

- Keep using the rear-facing car seat in the back seat of your car.
- Do not leave your baby alone in a high place or in the bath. Your baby is getting more active and can flip off table, bed, or countertop very quickly.
- Don't eat or drink hot items while holding your baby. Your baby is starting to grab at things and could get a bad burn.

ACTIVITIES TO HELP YOUR BABY'S DEVELOPMENT

- A few times a day, put your baby on his or her tummy when awake. This will help muscles develop, and your baby will learn to roll over.
- Let your baby play without any clothes on sometimes. A good place is on a towel in the middle of a double bed, with you right there. At 2 to 3 months, a baby likes being naked. Since the baby learns about the world largely through touching things, being naked lets your baby feel different textures. Being without clothes also lets the baby find his or her own body parts.
- Your baby likes looking at new things—and putting them into the mouth. Toys or objects of varying color, weight, and texture will stimulate your baby. You don't need anything fancy, but make sure that whatever your baby is playing with is safe.
- Hold your baby so he or she can see your face, and talk gently. When your baby responds in some way, answer back, as if you are having a real conversation.
- Continue to read, tell stories, and talk to your baby. Such activities can have dramatic effects on future learning.

CLINIC VISITS

The second immunizations for diphtheria-tetanus-pertussis, polio, and Hib are usually given at 4 months. If the first hepatitis B vaccine was given at 2 months, the second will be given at 3 or 4 months.

How do I keep my baby safe?

How can I help my baby develop?

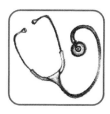

What immunizations will my baby need?

YOUR BABY: 4 MONTHS TO 6 MONTHS

YOUR BABY starts to get very active during these 2 months, learning to control more muscles, exploring the world more actively—and putting everything into the mouth.

NUTRITION

When will my baby start eating solid food?

- Breast milk or iron-fortified formula will give all of the nourishment your baby needs, but you may see signs that your baby is ready to try solid foods.
- Signs that your baby is ready for solid foods include:
  - suddenly taking more formula or nursing more;
  - waking up hungry in the middle of the night;
  - seeming to want to eat when others—you or other adults or children—are eating.
- A good first solid food is rice or oatmeal cereal. Start with about a tablespoon of dry cereal mixed with water, breast milk, formula, or non-citrus fruit juice (*not* orange juice) diluted with an equal amount of water.
- Some babies like their cereal thick, some like it thin. Experiment to see what your baby prefers.
- Between 4 to 8 tablespoons of dry cereal in one or two meals is a day's serving.
- After your baby has been eating cereal for a week or two, you can begin to try feeding pureed fruits and vegetables. Only do this if your baby seems to want more solids.
- Your baby should be nursing 4 to 6 times a day, or taking 20 to 35 ounces of formula a day.

ELIMINATION

- As your baby starts to eat solid foods, stools will change. If your baby has firmer stools, use oatmeal rather than rice cereal.
- Your baby's bladder is growing, and your baby won't need to urinate quite as often. You will not have to change diapers as often now, but they should be wetter when you do change them.
- All of your baby's feedings should be during the day now.

SLEEP

- Most babies now sleep about 10 hours through the night.
- If you haven't started a sleep routine for your baby, do it now. When your baby begins to look tired at night, get him or her ready for bed and put the baby in the crib while his or her eyes are open, so your baby can become familiar and comfortable with being in the crib and falling to sleep. Once your baby can go to sleep at the beginning of the night, he or she will be able to go back to sleep if wakened in the middle of the night.
- Naps vary. On average, your baby will take 3 naps during the day.

GROWTH AND DEVELOPMENT

- Your baby doesn't want to miss a minute of the world right now and may fuss when you put him or her on the tummy because it's harder to see.
- Most babies will learn to roll from front to back, and from back to front, during these months.
- Starting at about 3 months, babies need time to play independently, as well as to play with others.
- Your baby's reach is getting better, and everything will go into the mouth.
- With support, your baby can sit for a half hour or more.

What changes will I see in my baby?

SOCIAL

- Your baby is very social now, and enjoys seeing new places and new people. It's a good time to use babysitters, if you haven't already, because your baby is more likely to accept the occasional care of another person.
- Your baby is able to play alone now and needs some time to do that so he or she knows how to be alone.

SAFETY

- Keep using the rear-facing child seat in your car if your baby weighs less than 20 pounds dressed.
- Don't leave your baby alone in high places or in the bath.
- Start childproofing your house—your baby will be mobile soon. Go around your house at baby level and see what your baby will soon be able to get into. Are there uncovered outlets? Electric cords to pull? Breakable items just inside cabinet

How can I keep my baby safe?

doors? Heavy things that can be pulled or pushed over? Cleaning supplies, insecticides, drain cleaners, or other poisonous materials? For the next few years, you will need to adapt your home for the safety of your baby. Get dangerous items or materials out of reach—or out of the house altogether.

- Feed your baby solid food when he or she is strapped in a sturdy infant seat or chair.
- Be careful handling hot items around your baby; his or her hands are very quick to grab things now.
- Although your baby can use a walker, they are not recommended. It's too easy for a baby to roll one right down a flight of stairs.

ACTIVITIES TO HELP YOUR BABY'S DEVELOPMENT

- Lots of tummy time on the floor will help your baby develop upper body strength and learn to roll over. Your baby may fuss, though, when placed on the tummy.
- Jump-ups are fine for short periods, as long as your baby is not standing on his or her toes too much.
- Spend time looking into your baby's face and talking to him or her. Your baby will make sounds to try to keep your attention. Smile and talk as if you were having a conversation.

How can I help my baby develop?

- Give your baby safe objects and toys to grab, mouth, and shake. Show your baby different things to look at, from flowers in your garden to pictures on the wall.
- Your baby might be very interested in the sounds and images on television right now, but it's not good for your baby to spend too much time in front of the television. Infants need to be with real people who can respond to their needs and behaviors, not unresponsive images of people on a tv set.
- Reading simple infant books to your child continues to be instrumental to his or her intellectual development.

CLINIC VISITS

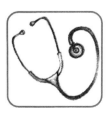

At 6 months, your baby will have another DTP and Hib vaccination. Depending on the schedule used, a third polio immunization and HBV vaccination may be given now also.

Babies 4 to 6 months
old enjoy grabbing and
mouthing things. Give your
baby a variety of safe objects
to explore. After 6 months, even
if your baby is not ready to walk,
he or she will try to pull to a
standing position to get a new
view of the world.

YOUR BABY: 6 MONTHS TO 10 MONTHS

YOUR BABY is learning to control his or her body and is becoming much more independent. From rolling over to crawling—even walking. From sucking on a finger to grabbing anything in reach. From the first smile and coo to a real word. All of these things are possible during these months.

Babies develop in different ways and at somewhat different rates. Your baby may be walking by 9 months—or barely crawling. Talk with your health care provider about how your baby is developing.

NUTRITION

- Solids are becoming as important as breast milk or formula. By 8 to 12 months, most babies are getting most of their nutrition through solid foods.
- When your baby can sit in a high chair and seems interested in what other people in the family are eating, you can start feeding soft table foods, rather than pureed baby foods.
- A good choice for your baby's first finger food is 1/4 of a graham cracker. It's easy to hold, and it dissolves quickly as the baby gums it.
- If your baby seems to gag on graham crackers or other soft table foods, wait a couple of weeks and then try again. Sometimes a baby just isn't interested yet, or the new texture is too strange. Some babies like new textures; others need to try something several times before they accept it.
- It's best to stick to a few new foods every few days so you don't overwhelm your baby.
- At about 7 or 8 months, try feeding your baby a regular Cheerio. If your baby can pick it up and eat it successfully, he or she is ready to try all soft table foods.
- A food is safe for your baby if it is about the size of a Cheerio and can be squeezed between your forefinger and thumb.
- By 9 to 10 months, your baby will be nursing 2 or 3 times a day or taking 16 to 24 ounces of formula.

ELIMINATION

- Stools continue to vary, depending on what you are feeding your baby. They are likely to have a stronger smell now, more like adult stools.
- It is not unusual to have a few stools per day some days, and none on others.

SLEEP

- Night routines are usually established and your baby should sleep 10 to 12 hours without waking.
- Nap patterns are now more regular, timed with meals. Two to three naps a day are common.
- Your baby will average about 14 hours of sleep a day.
- Between 6 and 12 months, your baby may wake at night. Give your baby a chance to go back to sleep without help.
- When your baby starts to grow teeth, gently brush them with plain water or wipe them with a cloth as part of the bedtime routine. This will help your child develop good toothbrushing habits as he or she grows.

GROWTH AND DEVELOPMENT

- Your baby will begin to sit without help, pull to a stand, crawl, and maybe even walk. The average age to walk is 12$1/2$ months.
- Your baby may begin saying some simple words around 8 to 10 months. "Mama," "dada," "bye-bye," and, of course, "no." At first these words will seem almost like accidents, but by 10 to 15 months, your baby probably will know how to use the simple words correctly.
- As your baby gets more active and more involved with the world, it's common for some fears to appear. A baby who always loved being bathed may develop a fear of water. A very sociable baby now only wants to be held by Mom. A baby who was eating solid foods pushes them away.

When will my baby start to walk?

What changes will I see in my baby?

SOCIAL

- Your baby likes to play, with you and others. Children this age like to watch other children play. If you have older children, they are likely to be your baby's favorite entertainment now.
- Boys begin to identify with men and older boys, girls with women and older girls.
- Your baby will have different moods, and will be more sensitive to the moods of other people. If you are upset, your baby is going to know it—and probably will get upset, too.
- Your baby's personality is getting stronger all the time. He or she likes some things, and not others. There may be a favorite toy, a favorite game, a favorite story, a favorite piece of music.
- As your baby learns more about the world, you need to teach what is okay and what is not. Instead of saying "no" all the time, try to give your baby something else to do or hold or play with. Set limits now on what your baby can do and what your baby can't do. For example, don't let your baby play with remote controls, telephones, or other things that are not toys and that you don't want your baby to play with in the future. If your baby grabs one of these items, give an acceptable toy or object instead and take away the wrong one.

SAFETY

- When your baby weighs 20 pounds in clothing, you can switch to a front-facing child seat in the car. The middle of the back seat is still the safest seating position.
- Put the mattress in your baby's crib at the lowest position, once your baby can get into a sitting position without help.
- Put the phone number for your local poison control center in a place where it is easy to see and use. Buy a bottle of ipecac and use only under the direction of the poison control center to make your baby vomit potentially poisonous substances.
- Once your baby can sit alone, try to avoid lightweight chairs or carriages that may tip over as your baby moves or shifts weight.

How do I keep my baby safe?

ACTIVITIES TO HELP YOUR BABY'S DEVELOPMENT

- Talk to your baby, face to face. Use simple words over and over, like your baby's name or a food or a special toy. Talk to your baby while you do things together. If you take your baby grocery shopping, talk about what foods you see on the shelf. Ask your baby to point to the peas, or the milk. Then point to it yourself.

- If you haven't been reading to your baby already, now is an important time to start. Even very small babies recognize the pictures and then the stories of their favorite books. Babies and small children like to hear the same story over and over again. That's how they learn to connect the words and the pictures to the story.

- Be dramatic. When you talk and play with your baby, use lots of different expressions, tones of voice, and movements of your hands and body.

- Give your baby room to move. A carpeted playroom floor is perfect, but not every family has that. In order to experiment with movements like rolling over, crawling, and walking, your baby needs a space without a lot of furniture or other things that can be tipped over or broken.

- Let your baby watch you do things. Babies at this age like to watch people do normal activities, like cooking, housework, and gardening. Find a safe thing your baby can do while you work. Give your baby a spoon to bang or a safe piece of food to play with while you cook. Let your baby crawl in the grass while you garden.

How can I help my baby develop?

CLINIC VISITS

Depending upon your clinic's schedule, your baby may have a check-up between 9 and 12months. Some clinics do the third Hepatitis B shot and may also check your baby's iron level, or hemoglobin, by taking a small sample of blood from your baby's finger.

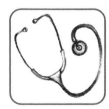

Exploring the outdoors is exciting for your toddler. Even on cold days, bundle up your baby and spend some time outside.

YOUR BABY: 10 MONTHS TO 15 MONTHS

YOUR BABY is becoming a toddler now, walking, eating solid foods, talking, and becoming more independent. Sometimes this can be hard, for you and your baby. Your baby has plenty of strong likes and dislikes, and can be very stubborn. But your baby needs you to set limits and to keep him or her safe. There are a lot of struggles between parents and children at this stage. Remember: You're the adult. You need to protect your child even as you let him or her know that it is okay to do some things independently.

NUTRITION

- By about a year old, most babies eat all soft table foods and want to feed themselves.
- Your baby can start using a cup now. You should try to have your baby off bottles by 12 to 15 months.
- If your baby is eating from all of the major food groups, you can replace formula with whole cow's milk.
- Your baby should eat mostly grains, such as cereal, bread, pasta, and rice, followed by fruits and vegetables and high-protein foods such as dairy products and meats. By a year old, 12 to 18 ounces of milk a day is enough.
- Small servings will encourage your baby to eat; you can always give more if your baby is still hungry.
- The correct servings for children this age are: a half-piece of bread, waffle, or bagel; 1/4 to 1/2 cup of cereal or pasta; one tablespoon of fruit, vegetable, or meat; 6 ounces of milk; 4 ounces of yogurt; 1 ounce or 1 slice of cheese.
- Using child-sized dishes, spoons, and forks helps your baby learn table skills. He or she will watch others to see how to use utensils.

ELIMINATION

- Stools and urine are usually predictable by now, although stools may change in frequency or consistency when new foods are introduced.

SLEEP

- Your baby may be so active that you will need to start a cooling-down period before bedtime, with quiet play to calm your baby.
- Naps should be consistent, usually 2 of them a day.
- Your baby will sleep about 15 hours a day.
- Clean your baby's teeth with water before bedtime.

GROWTH AND DEVELOPMENT

- Nearly all babies begin walking at this age.
- Your baby can use hands and fingers to grasp, throw, and drop things.
- Your baby understands many words and can follow simple commands.
- Babies are able to use at least simple words, and some babies will be able to talk quite a bit by 15 months. You should let your baby know that you are happy to hear his or her words.

SOCIAL

- Your baby's moods and preferences are obvious now, and sometimes a problem. Since your baby can also use the word "no," you may feel like you are in a struggle for control.
- Your baby is very sensitive to approval from others, especially you. While letting your baby know what he or she can do and what is not allowed, always show that you love your baby.
- "Separation anxiety" may show up, even with a baby who has been used to seeing lots of different people. You can help your baby understand that you will come back by practicing short separations and then coming back. Don't drag good-byes out when you leave your baby in daycare or with a babysitter; it only makes your baby more anxious. Say good-bye lovingly but firmly, then leave in a positive way.
- Teaching right from wrong is your main job as a parent now. Decide what is acceptable and what is not. You and others in the family should be united in how you deal with unacceptable behavior. If you don't want your baby to throw food, but your husband and older child simply laugh, your baby is going to be confused about what the rules are.

SAFETY

- Make sure your house is child-proofed, with gates on stairs, plugs in outlets, and latches on cabinet doors. Keep breakable items out of reach.
- Use a child-safety seat in your car at all times.
- Never leave your child alone near water.

ACTIVITIES TO HELP YOUR BABY'S DEVELOPMENT

- Give your baby a play space somewhere near where you usually are. A playroom in another part of the house is not as good as a space in the living room, next to where you are reading or cleaning.
- Let your baby explore the outdoors. Even in cold climates, a baby can be bundled up and taken outside to feel the snow or scuff through piles of fallen leaves. In good weather, there are hundreds of sights and sounds and things to feel.
- Talk to your child as you do things together. If you are cooking dinner, describe what you're doing in simple terms. If you are getting ready to give your baby a bath, list each body part as it is washed: "Now we wash your hand, now we wash your elbow, now we wash your shoulder...."
- Let your baby regularly play around other children of the same age. Although a child this young doesn't really play with others, he or she will learn a lot from watching other children, and will get used to the feeling of being with others. If your child is in daycare with other children, this is already a part of his or her life. But if your child is home with you and you have no other children, try to find an informal group of parents with other toddlers, or sign up for a parent-child class.

How can I help my baby develop?

CLINIC VISITS

Between 12 and 18 months, your child will get a DTAP and a Hib booster. During this same time, measles-mumps-rubella (MMR) and chicken pox vaccinations will be given. These last two immunizations protect your child from some dangerous illnesses that used to be common in childhood. An oral polio and a Hepatitis B shot may be given, depending on your clinic's immunization schedule.

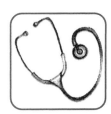

FOR PARTNERS

ALTHOUGH BABIES usually fix on their mothers first, they quickly become connected to others in their household who care for them. The more loving people who are in their life, the better off they will be.

Almost everything the baby's mother can do with the baby now can also be done by you. You can share the bathing and diapering and rocking. As the baby grows, you can share feeding.

Most important, you can share in activities that help the baby grow and develop. Talk to the baby, play with the baby, hold the baby.

When your baby is old enough to get around independently, you and your partner should agree on what kind of limits you want in your house, and then keep those limits consistent.

You and your partner need to spend time alone together. Sometimes that seems impossible with a small baby in the house. And sometimes mothers, especially if they are nursing, are reluctant to leave their babies even for a short time. You should encourage your partner to get out, with you and on her own, for some quality "adult" time. If you arrange for the child care, you can help make that evening out a reality.

FOR MORE INFORMATION

Taking Care of Your Child by Fries and Vickery Pantell.
Your Baby and Child: From Birth to Age Five by Penelope Leach.
The First Three Years of Life by Burton L. White.
The Magic Years by Selma Fraiberg.
Solve Your Child's Sleep Problems by Richard Ferber, MD
How to Get Your Kid to Eat ... But Not Too Much by E. Sutter.
The First Twelve Months of Life by T. Berry Brazelton.

Keeping Track of Your Baby

You may have a baby album to keep track of photographs and special moments in your baby's life, but these pages can help you work with your health care provider and give you a space to log a few of your baby's important developments.

YOU AND YOUR HEALTH CARE PROVIDER
QUESTIONS YOU HAVE ABOUT YOUR BABY'S DEVELOPMENT

When you think of something you want to remember to ask your health care provider, write it here. Take this book with you each time your baby goes to the clinic.

WHAT YOUR BABY IS DOING

It helps your health care provider if you keep track of your baby's regular eating, sleeping, and waking patterns:

How much does your baby sleep each day? When?
What is the longest time your baby sleeps?

How much does your baby nurse (or take bottles) every day?

What kind of stools does your baby have? How often?

How much does your baby cry? What kind of crying?

How much of the day is your baby alert?

Use this space to jot down anything that you think you might need to talk about.

CLINIC VISITS

Use this space to record each well-baby visit to your health care provider.

Date of visit

_____

Baby's height or length   Baby's weight

_____

Immunizations

_____

_____

Comments by health care provider about your baby's development

_____

_____

_____

_____

Date of visit

_____

Baby's height or length   Baby's weight

_____

Immunizations

_____

_____

Comments by health care provider about your baby's development

_____

_____

_____

_____

Date of visit

_____

Baby's height or length   Baby's weight

_____

Immunizations

_____

Comments by health care provider about your baby's development

_____

_____

_____

_____

Date of visit

_____

Baby's height or length   Baby's weight

_____

Immunizations

_____

Comments by health care provider about your baby's development

_____

_____

_____

_____

Date of visit

_____

Baby's height or length   Baby's weight

_____

Immunizations

_____

Comments by health care provider about your baby's development

_____

_____

_____

_____

Date of visit

_____

Baby's height or length   Baby's weight

_____

Immunizations

_____

_____

Comments by health care provider about your baby's development

_____

_____

_____

_____

Date of visit

_____

Baby's height or length   Baby's weight

_____

Immunizations

_____

_____

Comments by health care provider about your baby's development

_____

_____

_____

_____

Date of visit

_____

Baby's height or length   Baby's weight

_____

Immunizations

_____

_____

Comments by health care provider about your baby's development

_____

_____

_____

_____

Date of visit

_____

Baby's height or length   Baby's weight

_____

Immunizations

_____

Comments by health care provider about your baby's development

_____

_____

_____

_____

Date of visit

_____

Baby's height or length   Baby's weight

_____

Immunizations

_____

Comments by health care provider about your baby's development

_____

_____

_____

BABY'S FIRSTS

USE THIS SPACE to record some of the important—or fun—first times in your baby's life.

FIRST SMILE

Date

Smiled at …

Occasion

FIRST ROLLED OVER

Date

Occasion

FIRST LAUGHED

Date

Laughed at …

Occasion

FIRST HAIRCUT

Date

FIRST SAT UP

Date

FIRST STEPS ALONE

Date

_____

FIRST FAVORITE TOY

What was the toy?

_____

When did it became a favorite?

_____

FIRST WORD

Date

_____

To whom?

_____

What was the word?

_____

FIRST FRIEND

Name

_____

How did they become friends?

_____

What do they do together?

_____

FIRST COMPLETE SENTENCE

Date

_____

What was it?

_____

Occasion

_____

OTHER IMPORTANT FIRSTS

Index